THE SUPPOSED HEBRAISMS IN THE GRAMMAR OF THE BIBLICAL ARAMAIC

BY

HERBERT HARRY POWELL, PH.D.

WIPF & STOCK · Eugene, Oregon

Wipf and Stock Publishers
199 W 8th Ave, Suite 3
Eugene, OR 97401

The Supposed Hebraism in the Grammar of the Biblical Aramaic
By Powell, Herbert Harry
ISBN 13: 978-1-55635-798-5
Publication date 1/9/2008
Previously published by University of California, 1907

The following paper was written under the direction of Professor Max L. Margolis, Ph.D., and presented to the Faculty of the University of California in partial satisfaction of the requirements for the degree of Doctor of Philosophy, which was granted in May, 1905. Inasmuch as Dr. Margolis has since severed his connection with the University, I take this opportunity of expressing my deep sense of obligation to him not only for his wealth of suggestion, counsel, and inspiration, but also for the generous use of his own private library, without which these studies would have been impossible.

H. H. P.

San Mateo, California,
November, 1906.

The following paper [illegible] dissertation [illegible] Max L. Margolis, Ph.D., [illegible] to the Faculty of the University of California [illegible] Dr. Margolis [illegible] and [illegible]

A. H. [illegible]

ABBREVIATIONS

AJSL: *American Journal of Semitic Languages.*

Baer: *Libri Danielis, Ezrae et Nehemiae* (Leipzig, 1882).

Barth, *Nomin.:* *Die Nominalbildung in den semitischen Sprachen* (Leipzig, 1889–91).

Behrmann: *Das Buch Daniel* (Göttingen, 1894).

Bevan: *A Short Commentary on the Book of Daniel* (Cambridge, 1892).

Brockelmann: *Syrische Grammatik* (Berlin, 1899).

BSS: *Beiträge zur Assyriologie und vergleichenden semitischen Sprachwissenschaft.*

CIS: *Corpus Inscriptionum Semiticarum.*

Cooke: *A Text-Book of North Semitic Inscriptions* (Oxford, 1903).

Dalman: *Grammatik des jüdisch-palästinischen Aramäisch* (Leipzig, 1894).

Del. *Assyr. Gr.:* Delitzsch, *Assyrian Grammar* (Berlin, 1889).

Del. *HW:* Delitzsch, *Assyrisches Handwörterbuch* (Leipzig, 1896).

Driver: *Introduction to the Literature of the Old Testament*, 8th ed. (New York, 1898).

Driver, *Tenses:* *A Treatise on the Use of the Tenses in Hebrew* (Oxford, 1892).

EB: Cheyne and Black, *Encyclopaedia Biblica.*

Enc. Brit.: *Encyclopaedia Britannica.*

Graf: *Der Prophet Jeremia erklärt* (1862).

Ginsb.: Ginsburg, *The Massoretico-Critical Text of the Hebrew Bible* (London, 1894).

GK: Gesenius-Kautzsch, *Hebrew Grammar* (Oxford, 1898).

JA: *Journal Asiatique.*

JAOS: *Journal of the American Oriental Society.*

Jahn: *Das Buch Daniel* (Leipzig, 1904).

JE: *Jewish Encyclopedia* (New York).

JHU Circ.: *Johns Hopkins University Circulars* (Baltimore).

JQR: *Jewish Quarterly Review* (London).

Kautzsch: *Grammatik des Biblisch-Aramäischen* (Leipzig, 1884).

Kautzsch *Aramaismen:* *Die Aramaismen im Alten Testament;* I, Lexikalischer Teil (Halle, 1902).

König: *Lehrgebäude der hebräischen Sprache* (Leipzig, 1881).

Lagarde: *Mittheilungen* (Göttingen, 1891).

Lagarde: *Übersicht über die im Aramäischen, Arabischen, und Hebräischen übliche Bildung der Nomina* (Göttingen, 1889).

Lidz.: Lidzbarski, *Handbuch der nordsemitischen Epigraphik* (Weimar, 1898).

Lindberg: *Vergleichende Grammatik der semitischen Sprachen* (Goteburg, 1897).

Marti: "Das Buch Daniel," in *Kurzer Hand-Commentar zum Alten Testament* (Tübingen und Leipzig, 1901).

Marti, *Gram.:* *Kurzgefasste Grammatik der Biblisch-Aramäischen Sprache* (Berlin, 1896).

Nestle: *Marginalien und Materialien* (Tübingen, 1893).

Nöldeke: *Kurzgefasste syrische Grammatik*, 2d ed. (Leipzig, 1898).

Nöldeke, *Mand.:* *Mandäische Grammatik* (Halle, 1875).

Praetorius: *Aethiopische Grammatik* (Berlin, 1886).

PRE: *Realencyclopädie für protestantische Theologie und Kirche*, 3d ed.

PS: R. Payne Smith, *Thesaurus Syriacus* (Oxford, 1879).

REJ: *Revue des Études Juives.*

Riessler: *Das Buch Daniel* (Wien, 1902).

SBOT: *The Sacred Books of the Old Testament:* a critical edition of the Hebrew Text, printed in colors, with notes, under the editorial direction of Paul Haupt (Baltimore, Ezra, 1901; Dan, 1896).

Sievers: *Grundzüge der Phonetik*, 3d ed. (Leipzig, 1885).
Spitta: *Grammatik des arabischen Vulgardialectes von Aegypten* (Leipzig, 1880).
Stade: *Lehrbuch der hebräischen Grammatik* (Leipzig, 1879).
Strack: *Grammatik des biblischen Aramäisch*, 4th ed. (Leipzig, 1905).
Vernier: Le P. Donat Vernier, S. J., *Grammaire Arabe* (Beyrouth, 1901).
Vollers-Burkitt: *The Modern Egyptian Dialect of Arabic* (Cambridge, 1895).
Wellhausen: *Skizzen und Vorarbeiten* (Berlin, 1899).
Wright: *Arabic Grammar*, 3d ed. (Cambridge, 1896).
Wright: *Comparative Grammar of the Semitic Languages* (Cambridge, 1890).
WZKM: *Wiener Zeitschrift für die Kunde des Morgenlandes.*
ZA: *Zeitschrift für Assyriologie.*
ZAW: *Zeitschrift für alttestamentliche Wissenschaft.*
ZDMG: *Zeitschrift der deutschen morgenländischen Gesellschaft.*
Zimmern: *Vergleichende Grammatik der semitischen Sprachen* (Berlin, 1898).

SUMMARY OF CONTENTS

Introduction

II. MORPHOLOGY

UNIVERSITY OF CALIFORNIA PUBLICATIONS

SEMITIC PHILOLOGY

Vol. 1, No. 1, pp. 1–55 February, 1907

THE SUPPOSED HEBRAISMS IN THE GRAMMAR OF THE BIBLICAL ARAMAIC

BY

HERBERT HARRY POWELL, PH.D.

1. By Biblical Aramaic we understand the language of Gen. 31, 47 (two words); Jer. 10, 11; Dan. 2, 4*b*–7, 28; and Ezra 4, 8–6, 18; 7, 12–26.[a]

The date of some of these documents is disputed,[b] but with reference to the bulk of the records[c] we may speak of BA as the vernacular speech of the Jews[d] in the Persian and Greek periods of their history. While, therefore, later than the Zenjirli inscriptions, they antedate all other Aramaic records, notably the very extensive Christian literature in the Edessene commonly called Syriac.

[a] The Aramaic words and phrases in the New Testament are not treated here. For a detailed examination of them, see Kautzsch, § 5, 2, *a* and *b;* Dalman, 1894, *passim* (see Greek index).

[b] Although found in a portion from E., Gen. 31, 47 is regarded as a gloss by Wellhausen, *Composition des Hexateuchs*, 1889, 43, and Dillmann, II, 265. Jer. 10, 11, which interrupts the connection between vv. 10 and 12, is thrown out by Graf (p. 160) and others as a marginal note; its date is necessarily posterior to that of 10, 1–16, which is the work of a writer who consciously imitates the language of Deutero-Isaiah (see Giesebrecht's Commentary, 1894, 62; Cornill, *SBOT.*, 1895, 74).

[c] The Aramaic document used by the compiler of Ezra probably formed part of a narrative of the rebuilding of the Temple. It seems to have been trustworthy, although its extent is a matter of conjecture; its scope may have been more or less comprehensive. At the points where the document was inserted into the compilation, the Aramaic verses establishing the connection belong to the Chronicler; possibly they were found by him in a compilation previously made. Cf. Driver,

Introd., 549; Bertholet's Commentary, 1902, xiv f. Doubt has been cast on the authenticity of the edicts (notably by Kosters, 1895; Wellhausen, 1895), though perhaps without sufficient foundation (see E. Meyer, *Entstehung des Judenthums*, 1896); it is probable, however, that the present form was given to the edicts by the Chronicler or some previous compiler. (See, for a review of the question, J. Fischer, *Die chronologischen Fragen in den Büchern Esra-Nehemia*, 1903, 4 ff.)

As for the book of Daniel, internal evidence makes it certain that it was written in Palestine during the persecutions of Antiochus Epiphanes, B. C. 168 or 167. See Bevan, 1–25; Behrmann, XVI–XXII; and, for a more conservative estimate, Driver's Commentary in the Cambridge Bible, 1901, Introduction, § 3.

The bilingual character of the book has been variously explained: (1) The Aramaic portion represents old Aramaic writings worked over and fitted into the framework of the book in Maccabean times (Spinoza, as cited by Kamphausen, *EB.*, col. 1004; and in a somewhat different form Meinhold, cited by Driver and Marti). (2) The whole book was originally written in Aramaic, and then certain parts which had been lost were replaced from a Hebrew translation (Huetius, cited by Kamphausen, *EB.*, *ibid.*). (3) The whole book was originally composed in Aramaic, and the beginning and the ending were subsequently translated into Hebrew in order to secure for the book a place in the sacred canon (Marti, IX f.). (4) The whole book was originally written in Hebrew, but a part was destroyed and then replaced from an Aramaic translation, which perhaps was the work of the author himself (Bevan, 27, following Lenormant; Haupt, Daniel, *SBOT.*, 16). (5) The author "evidently fell into the error of regarding 'Chaldean' as the language of Babylonia," and then continued writing in that language because "he was so familiar with both languages that he could glide from one into the other without noticing it, and could assume for a great portion of his contemporaries a knowledge of them both" (Kamphausen, *EB.*, col. 1005; so also Driver and Behrmann).

It is maintained (Riessler, § 1; Jahn, V) that the LXX translator had before him a Hebrew text of the Aramaic section. The examples enumerated by Jahn (*ibid.*, footnote 1) in support of his thesis, however, are not conclusive. With the exception of two passages (7, 8; 2, 44), the argument is based upon so-called Greek "Hebraisms." In 7, 8 ἐξήρθησαν stands for ἐξηράνθησαν; cf. Zech. 10, 2, where ℵ[c.b] have the correct reading ἐξήρθησαν for ἐξηράνθησαν, which the other codices offer, and Sir. 10, 17, where again ℵAC, several cursives, and the Ethiopic and Sahidic versions read ἐξῆρεν (Heb. וסחם, read וַיִּסָּחֵם) instead of the ἐξήρανεν of B and the Latin (see Nestle, *Marginalien*, 50); cf. also in Jer. 28 (51), 36, ξηρανῶ AB for ἐξαρῶ ℵ. In 2, 44 LXX reads

תִּשְׁבֻּק for תִּשְׁתְּבֻק. The opinion that the Aramaic section goes back to a Hebrew original is rejected by Marti, p. x.

[d] The fact that the Palestinian Jews spoke Aramaic is certainly undeniable. Even before the Exile the language was understood by the princes of Judah, although it was unintelligible to the common people (II Kings 18, 26). Some of the colonists brought into Palestine to take the place of the exiled Israelites were from Aramaic regions, e. g., Hamath (*ibid.*, 17, 24). As the national life of the Jews weakened, it became increasingly difficult for them to resist the encroachments of the Aramaic language spoken by their neighbors, which steadily grew to be the language of everyday life. In the eighth and seventh centuries B. C. Aramaic was used even in Babylonia and Assyria along with the native speech. We must "not for a moment suppose that the Jews lost the use of Hebrew in the Babylonian captivity, and brought back with them into Palestine this so-called Chaldee. The Aramean dialect, which gradually got the upper hand since the fourth or fifth century B. C., did not come that long journey across the Syrian desert; it was *there*, on the spot; and it ended by taking possession of the field, side by side with the kindred dialect of the Samaritans" (Wright, *Comp. Gram.*, 16). On the displacement of Hebrew by Aramaic cf. Kautzsch, § 4; Nöldeke, *Enc. Brit.*, XXI, 648.

2. The Aramaic portions of the Old Testament have come down to us in the same square characters,[a] and are furnished with the same vowel and accent symbols,[b] as the Hebrew portions of the Bible. The problem at once arises: How far was the Masoretic system, developed for the Hebrew of the Old Testament, applied also to the Aramaic portions? Hebrew influence of this character would, if found, be placed to the credit of the schools of the readers and masters of the late synagogue. Quite different is the following question: To what extent was BA, as the living speech of the post-exilic Jewish community in Palestine, influenced by the Hebrew which still continued to be used in school and synagogue even after it had been supplanted in the daily life of the people?[c] Here the case is much analogous to the problem of Hebraisms in Biblical Greek,[d] except for the following facts: first, that Hebrew and Aramaic are cognate languages, and therefore more liable to influence each other; secondly, that the Greek texts of the Bible are mainly translations,[e] while the Aramaic texts are originals.[f]

[a] The so-called square characters in which our MSS. of the Hebrew Bible are written are not Hebrew in origin, but Aramaic. They represent the forms which the old Hebrew alphabet (= Phœnician, Western Semitic in general) assumed, through gradual transformation in the course of centuries, in the Aramaic (Egyptian and Palmyrene). The question still remains whether this transformation from old to square was gradual in the case of the Biblical text, as it was in ordinary documents, or whether the change was deliberate and was made by an authoritative body long after the new characters had established themselves in common use. Tradition (Jewish, in the Talmud, verified by references in the church fathers) ascribes the change to Ezra. Jewish coins down to the time of Bar Kokhba bear the old characters. The notice found in the church fathers that in Greek versions the Tetragrammaton was written in Hebrew and in the old characters, is now verified by the Cairene fragment of Aquila (ed. Burkitt, 1897; see the discussion on p. 15 f. [the spelling with י in place of ו—יהיה for יהוה—is on a line with אלדים, אלקים, according to Margolis]). Cf., on the whole subject, Driver, *Hebrew Text of Samuel*, 1890, XVII–XXV; Lidzbarski, 189 ff.; and art. Alphabet in *JE.*, I, 442 f., especially p. 445, col. 2, and Plates I–III.

[b] On the value of the vocalization in Daniel see Bevan, 33 f.; Nöldeke, *EB.*, col. 282; and contrast Kamphausen, *EB.*, col. 1005; König, *JE.*, IV, 430 f. During the last half-century another system of vowel symbols has been brought to light. It is known as the superlinear, since the vowel signs are all written above the consonants. Two MSS. are cited by Strack (*GBA.*, 4) for Daniel: one, the Codex Jamanensis, of little value, containing chapters 1, 8—2, 49, and 4, 21—7, 7; the other, Codex Derenburgii, containing all of the Aramaic of Daniel except 2, 28–41; 4, 5–22; 6, 27—7, 4 and 7, 15–20. On this system of vocalization, see G. Margoliouth, *International Congress of Orientalists*, IX, 1893, 46–56; and cf. *Proceedings of the Society of Biblical Archaeology*, Feb. 1893, Vol. XV, part 4; Neubauer, *JQR.*, VII (1895), 361 f.; Friedländer, *ibid.*, 564 ff.; Bacher, *ZDMG.*, XLIX (1895), 15 f.; Barnstein, *Targum of Onkelos to Genesis*, 1896, 6 f. and especially 14 ff.; Levias, *AJSL.*, XV (1899), 157 ff.; Praetorius, *ZDMG.*, LIII (1899), 181 ff.; Kahle, *ZAW.*, XXI (1901), 273 ff.; GK, 39, n. 1.

[c] On mixture in languages, see Whitney, *Transactions of American Philological Association*, 1881; Paul, *Prinzipien der Sprachgeschichte*, 1898, c. xxii, especially §§ 276, 283 ff.; Sweet, *History of Language*, 1900, 81–96. The general opinion is that the pronunciation and syntax, rather than the morphology, are affected by the mixture.

[d] On the Hebraisms of Biblical Greek see Deissmann, *Bibelstudien* (1895); *Neue Bibelstudien* (1897); *Die sprachliche Erforschung d. griech. Bibel* (1898); his article in *PRE.*, VII (1899), 62 ff.; Thumb, *Die griechische Sprache im Zeitalter des Hellenismus*, 1901, 12 ff.;

cf. also Grenfell-Hunt-Smyly, *Tebtunis Papyri*, I (1902), 86 (n. 14). Many of the supposed Hebraisms have been found to be part of the common Hellenistic language.

[e] That some of the New Testament books (Gospels and Acts) bear the impress of being translations from a Semitic original was noted by Spinoza, who observes (*Tractatus theologico-politicus*, c. vii) that "quamvis aliis linguis vulgati fuerint (libri N. T.), hebraizant tamen .... Ev. enim secundum Matt. et sine dubio etiam epistola ad Hebr. Hebraice ex communi opinione scripta sunt, quae tamen non extant." Recently the question has been reopened; see Nestle, *Philologica Sacra* (1896); Dalman, *Die Worte Jesu* (1898); Wellhausen, *Skizzen*, VI (1899), 188–194.

[f] See, however, above, § 1, c.

3. The question of grammatical Hebraisms in BA has been adverted to by grammarians and commentators.[a] It appears that Kautzsch is isolated in his assumption of strong traces of Hebrew influence in BA; all other scholars who have expressed opinions are inclined to regard the so-called Hebraisms as remnants of an older linguistic stage in which Aramaic was still nearer to the Hebrew. A fresh investigation of the subject based upon as complete an induction as possible, especially as regards the inscriptional material, as well as upon a fuller discussion of rival opinions and, it is believed, a more adequate weighing of the evidence presented by the phenomena of general Semitic grammar, is attempted in the following pages, and built upon the following canons of elimination:

A. An agreement between BA and Hebrew found in the non-Jewish Aramaic dialects must be eliminated from the list of possible Hebraisms.

B. An agreement between BA and Hebrew occasioned by the fact of their relationship within the class of Semitic languages must be similarly eliminated.

C. An agreement between BA and Hebrew due to Aramaic influence upon Hebrew can have no place in our list.

Whatever agreements are left, not covered by these canons, may be ascribed to Hebrew influence.

[a] G. B. Winer, *Grammatik des biblischen und targum. Chaldaismus*, 1824, 5 f., rejects the opinion that BA was from the beginning a corrupt and mixed jargon, and maintains that it bears the character of a real Aramaic dialect. He considers the few agreements with

Hebrew as against Syriac, which are confined almost entirely to orthography and vocalization, as dialectal differences rather than mutuations introduced from the Hebrew by the schools of the Jewish punctators, since the identical pronunciation of Aramaic is attested by the Greek transcription of Aramaic words in the N. T.

Renan, *Histoire générale des langues sémitiques*,[4] 1863, 220 f., agrees with Winer on the one hand against Hupfeld, who considers the BA as a Jewish jargon, and on the other against Dietrich, who interprets the so-called Hebraisms as elements of primitive Aramaic, in maintaining that BA is an Aramaic dialect "légèrement hébraïsé." He regrets the lack of non-Jewish Aramaic documents which renders a conclusive opinion difficult. As examples of Hebrew influences he cites ה for א, the Hoph'al, and segolate forms.

S. D. Luzzatto, *Elementi grammaticali del Chaldeo Biblico*, 1865 (German trans., 1873), § 2, assumes the existence of Hebraisms. See esp. §§ 3, 16, 43, 81, 107.

E. Kautzsch, § 8, asserts that BA bears strong traces of Hebrew influence. "These Hebraisms, however," he continues, "may be attributed in large part to late copyists who either through ignorance or through design conformed their texts to the rules of Hebrew grammar." Kautzsch's views in detail will be found referred to in the course of the present work.

M. J. de-Goeje, in a review of Kautzsch's *Grammar* (*Theologisch Tijdschrift*, XIX (1885), 70), warns against being "te rasch met de aanname van Hebraïsmen in het Arameesch van het O. T." Cf. Nöldeke, in *GGA*, 1884, No. 26, 1015.

A. A. Bevan, Commentary, 38 f., has the following to say on our question: "A very difficult and much debated question is how far BA was influenced by Hebrew. As a rule, philologists were formerly inclined to go very far in assuming the existence of Hebraisms, but many of the linguistic phenomena which were so regarded have been proved by recent discoveries to be genuine Aramaic." He mentions, however, some undeniable Hebraisms; his opinion will be adverted to later on.

G. Behrmann, Commentary, p. viii, correctly defines the so-called Hebraisms of the BA as remnants of an older stage of the language in which Aramaic was still nearer to Hebrew. He also rightly eliminates Masoretic peculiarities which have no foundation in the consonantal text.

A. AGREEMENTS BETWEEN BA AND HEBREW FOUND ALSO IN THE NON-JEWISH[a] ARAMAIC DIALECTS

4. Aramaic is one of the North Semitic languages, and, in the course of its history, was spoken throughout Mesopotamia, Syria, and Palestine.[b] Upon the decay of Babylonian culture

and influence, Aramaic became the international language of commerce and diplomacy (II Kings 18, 26). The oldest specimens of Aramaic are the inscriptions from Zenjirli, Nineveh and Babylon, which belong to the eighth and seventh centuries almost all the others being from Persian times or later (cf. Lidzbarski, 121). The distribution of the inscriptions[c] according to place and time appears as follows:

1. Zenjirli, eighth and seventh centuries B. C.[d]
2. Nerab, seventh century B. C.
3. Babylon, about 700 B. C.
4. Tema, fifth and fourth centuries B. C.
5. Egypt, fifth century B. C. and later.
6. Nabatea, 9 B. C. to 94 A. D.
7. Palmyra, first to third centuries A. D.

[a] We leave out of account the Jewish and Samaritan Aramaic writings, because they are likely to show Hebraisms, and because we have as yet no reliable edition of the Targums with vowel-points (cf. Merx, *International Congress of Orientalists*, Berlin (1881), I, 142–225). The Jewish Aramaic is represented by the Targums, which, however, did not receive their present form until a comparatively late date. The Samaritan dialect is represented by the translation of the Pentateuch. The Christian Palestinian dialect, likewise, was probably affected by Hebrew influence; hence it is omitted from our discussion.

[b] On the geographical area of Aramaic see Kautzsch, § 1; Nöldeke, *EB.*, cols. 280 ff.; GK., §§ 1, 2 and the literature there mentioned. On Assyrian as an older local variety of Aramaic, see JHU. circulars, No. 114, July, 1894, 118b. On the Arameans generally, see McCurdy, *History, Prophecy and the Monuments*, I, 24, 71, 84, 244, 408, and III, p. 26.

[c] Most of the Aramaic inscriptions are contained in the *Corpus Inscriptionum Semiticarum*, part second, Paris, 1889. Unless otherwise noted, all references to these inscriptions are to the numbers in the *Corpus*.

[d] The inscriptions from Zenjirli, a small village in northwest Syria, afford the earliest specimens extant of Aramaic. They were discovered in 1890 and 1891. Although undoubtedly Aramaic, the dialect has features which ally it to Hebrew. It is just with reference to this affinity of the Zenjirli inscriptions with Hebrew that Sachau (quoted by Behrmann, p. viii, footnote) remarks that the older the Aramaic is, the more it is like Hebrew. On these inscriptions see Lidzbarski, 440 f.; Cooke, 185; Halévy, *JA.*, XIX (1892), VIII; Nöldeke, *ZDMG.*, XLVIII (1893), 96 f.; D. H. Müller, *WZKM.*, VII (1893), 113 ff.; X (1896), 193 ff.; Hoffmann, *ZA.*, XI (1897).

5. Among the remnants of Aramaic[a] BA belongs chronologically between Egyptian Aramaic and the language of the Nabatean inscriptions. They all belong to the Western group of dialects, the Eastern[b] being represented by the Syriac,[c] or dialect of Edessa, the Mandaic, and the language of the Babylonian Talmud. The Mohammedan conquest replaced Aramaic as the vernacular with Arabic, the former surviving in Syria and Persia only in certain isolated and more or less corrupt dialects.[d]

[a] For a more comprehensive and detailed list of these remnants, see Kautzsch, § 5; Zimmern, § 1, *c;* on their comparative value for philological purposes, see Nöldeke, *EB.*, col. 284.

[b] The Western branch of Aramaic differs from the Eastern chiefly in the prefix of the 3rd sing. masc. imperf., which is *i̥*. In Syriac the prefix is *n*, which is also usual in Mandaic. The Babylonian Talmud sometimes has *n*, but more commonly *l*. See Bevan, 33 f.; Behrmann, p. vi; Wright, *Comp. Gram.*, 19.

[c] From the third to the seventh century A. D., Syriac produced an extensive ecclesiastical literature. It developed also systems of vowel symbols by which the pronunciation was more or less accurately represented. After being supplanted by Arabic as the vernacular, it remained in use for a long time in monasteries and schools as a literary and ecclesiastical language. See Nöldeke, pp. xxxi–xxxiv; and *EB.*, cols. 284, 285; Wright, *Syriac Literature*, 1894; Merx, *Historia artis grammaticae apud Syros*, 1889.

[d] On the modern Syriac dialects of Persia, see Stoddard, "Grammar of Modern Syriac as spoken in Oroomia, Persia and Koordistan," *JAOS.*, V (1856), 1–183; A. J. Maclean in *Intern. Cong. of Oriental.*, IX, London (1892), 33–45, and *Grammar of the Dialects of Vernacular Syriac*, Cambridge, 1895. On the dialect of Ma'lula in Syria, see Ferrette, *Journal of the Royal Asiatic Society* (old series), XX (1863), 431 f.; Renan, *Histoire générale*, 268; Nöldeke, *ZDMG.*, XXI (1867), 183 f.; Merx, *ZDMG.*, XXII (1868), 271 f.; Socin, *ZDMG.*, XXIV (1870), 229 f.; Prym, *ZDMG.*, XXV (1871), 652; Merx, *JA.*, Series VII, XII (1878), 178 f., and XIII (1879), 165 f.; Parisot, *JA.*, Series IX, XI (1898), 239–312, 440–519; XII (1899), 124–176. On the dialect of Ṭur-'Abdin see Prym and Socin, *Der neu-aramäische Dialekt des Ṭûr-'Abdīn*, Göttingen, 1881, and the review by Nöldeke, *ZDMG.*, XXXV (1881), 218–235; also Parisot, *International Congress of Orientalists*, Paris, 1897, 179–198.

6. BA differs from Syriac and agrees with Hebrew orthographically in the use of ה where Syriac has א (ܐ). Similarly,

certain words are written with שׂ, where Syriac has ס (ܣ), the letter שׂ not being found in Syriac.

The irregularity in the use of ה and א appears in:

a) The ending of the emphatic state of nouns.

b) The ending of the absolute state of feminine nouns.

c) The ending of infinitives.

d) Pronouns.

e) Pronominal suffixes.

f) Verbs ל״א (ל״י).

a) Masculine nouns and adjectives in the emphatic state are written with א in the following examples (the asterisk * marking forms which appear with both ה and א): אַבְנָא 2, 35; 5, 4. 23; אַזְדָּא (if we accept the view of Andreas, in Marti, *Gramm.*, 51*, who derives it from Middle Persian *azd;* on the reading see note in Ginsburg's Bible) 2, 5. 8; אִילָנָא 4, 8. 11. 17. 20. 23; אֱלָהָא 34 times; אַלְפָּא 5, 1; אנושא (k), אֲנָשָׁא (ḳ) 4, 13. 14; אֲנָשָׁא 2, 38 + 9 times; אֱסָרָא 6, 9. 10. 14; אָעָא 5, 4. 23; אַרְגְּוָנָא 5, 7. 16. 29; אַרְעָא 2, 35 + 19 times (in 2, 39 k has ארעא and ḳ ארע; here the word is used adverbially); אַרְקָא Jer. 10, 11; אַתּוּנָא 3, 19. 22; *בַּיְתָא Ez. 5, 3. 9. 11; 6, 3; בִּנְיָנָא Ez. 5, 4; בָּרָא 4, 9 + 6 times; בִּשְׂרָא 2, 11; 4, 9; גַּבָּא 6, 17 + 6 times; גִּירָא 5, 5; *דַּהֲבָא 2, 35 + 12 times; *דִּינָא 7, 10. 22. 26; דָּתָא 2, 13. 15; Ez. 7, 12. 21. 26; דִּתְאָא 4, 12. 20 (in 4, 20 Ginsb. gives דתאה as a var.); הַדְרָא 5, 18; הֵיכְלָא 5, 2 + 8 times; המינכא (k) הַמְנִיכָא (ḳ) 5, 7. 16. 29; זִמְנָא 3, 7. 8; 4, 33; 7, 22; Ez. 5, 3; זְמָרָא 3, 5. 7. 10. 15; חֲבָלָא Ez. 4, 22; חַיָּא 6, 21. 27; חֶזְוָא 2, 19; חֶלְמָא 2, 4 + 16 times; חֲמָרָא 5, 1. 2. 4. 23; חִסְנָא 2, 37; חֲסַפָּא 2, 34. 35. 43. 45; חֲשׁוֹכָא 2, 22; טוּרָא 2, 45; טִינָא 2, 41. 43; טַעְמָא 6, 3; Ez. 4, 21; 5, 5; יוֹמָא 6, 11. 14; יַמָּא 7, 2. 3; *יְקָרָא 2, 37; 5, 18; יַקִּירָא Ez. 4, 10; כָּהֲנָא Ez. 7, 12. 21; כַּסְפָּא 2, 35 + 9 times; כָּרוֹזָא 3, 4; כשדיא (k) 5, 30; *כְּתָבָא 5, 8 + 7 times; לֵילְיָא 2, 19; 5, 30; 7, 2. 7. 13; מֹאזַנְיָא 5, 27; מדיא (k) 6, 1; מַדְבְּחָא Ez. 7, 17 (Ginsb. gives a var. מדבחה); *מַלְכָּא 2, 4 + 155 times; מַנְדְּעָא 2, 21; מִשְׁתְּיָא 5, 10; נְבִיָּא (ḳ) Ez. 5, 1; 6, 14; נָגְהָא 6, 20; נהירא (k) נהורא (ḳ) 2, 22; נוּרָא 3, 6 + 12 times; *נַהֲרָא Ez. 4, 16; נְחָשָׁא 2, 35 + 4 times; נִשְׁתְּוָנָא Ez. 4, 18, 23; 5, 5; סוֹפָא 6, 27; 7, 26. 28; סִפְרָא Ez. 4, 8. 9. 17. 23; עִדָּנָא 2, 8. 9; 3, 5. 15; עֵטָא 2, 14; עליא (k) 3, 26 + 9 times; עָלְמָא 2, 20 + 5 times; *עַמָּא Ez. 7, 13. 16. 25 (in 7, 13 Ginsb. gives a var. עַמָּה); עִשְׂבָּא 4, 22. 29. 30; 5, 21; פַּסָּא 5, 24; פַּרְזְלָא 2, 34 + 11 times; פרסיא (k) 6, 29; *פִּשְׁרָא 2, 4 + 7 times; פִּתְגָמָא 4, 14, Ez.

4, 17; 5, 7. 11; 6, 11; צַלְמָא 2, 31 + 7 times; קַרְנָא 3, 5 + 7 times; רַבָּא 7, 2; Ez. 4, 10; 5, 8; רביעיא (k) 2, 40; 3, 25; 7, 7. 23; רוּחא 2, 35; רָזָא 2, 18 + 4 times; שְׁאָרָא 7, 7. 19; שַׁבִּיבָא 3, 22; שָׁלְטָנָא 7, 27; שַׁלִּיטָא 2, 15; שְׁלָמָא Ez. 5, 7; שִׁמְשָׁא 6, 15; שְׁפַרְפָּרָא 6, 20; *תְּלָתָא Ez. 6, 4; תַּלְתָּא 5, 16, 29; תָּקְפָּא 2, 37. Also the adverbs אַדְרַזְדָּא Ez. 7, 23; אָסְפַּרְנָא Ez. 5, 8 + 6 times; the not altogether certain form אֻשַּׁרְנָא Ez. 5, 3. 9, and the proper name דּוּרָא 3, 1.

Masculine nouns in the emphatic state occur with ה as follows: *בַּיְתָה Ez. 5, 12; 6, 15; *דַּהֲבָה Ez. 5, 14; 6, 5; 7, 18; *דִּינָה Ez. 7, 26; דִּכְרוֹנָה Ez. 6, 2; *יַקִּירָה 5, 20; כַּשְׂדָּאָה (k) 5, 30; Ez. 5, 12; *כְּתָבָה 5, 7. 15; מָדָאָה (k) 6, 1; *מַלְכָּה 2, 11; נביאה (k) Ez. 5, 1; 6, 14; *נַהֲרָה Ez. 5, 3 + 12 times in Ezra; עִלָּאָה (k) 3, 26. 32; 5, 18. 21; *עַמָּה Ez. 5, 12; פָּרְסָאָה (k) 6, 29; *פִּשְׁרָה 2, 7; 5, 12; רְבִיעָאָה (k) 2, 40; 3, 25; 7, 7. 23; רֵאשָׁה 2, 38; *תַּלְתָּה 3, 24 + 5 times. Note that ה is the rule when, as in the marginal forms (k) noted, it is preceded by א. The ה in these cases is to be regarded as purely orthographic, and presupposes spellings like כַּשְׂדָּא, which latter, in accordance with general Semitic usage, is for כַּשְׂדָּאָא (cf. below, § 38).

The masculine plural emphatic state ends everywhere in ־ַיָּא (or ־ֵא), except in the single instance שׁוּרַיָּה Ez. 4, 16. Most probably, however, the vocalization in this instance is wrong, שׁוּרַיַּהּ having been intended by the writer (so LXX, III Ez. 2, 20, Peshiṭta).

Feminine nouns in the emphatic state singular with א are as follows: אִגַּרְתָּא Ez. 4, 11; 5, 6; בְּאִישְׁתָּא Ez. 4, 12; בִּירְתָא Ez. 6, 2; גְּבוּרְתָא 2, 20, 23; גָּלוּתָא 2, 25; 5, 13; 6, 14; Ez. 6, 16; חֵיוְתָא 4, 12 + 5 times (in 4, 11 Ginsb. gives a var. חֵיוְתָה); חָכְמְתָא 2, 20. 21. 23; יַבֶּשְׁתָּא 2, 10; יְקִדְתָּא 3, 6 + 7 times; מְדִינְתָּא Ez. 5, 8; 6, 2; *מַלְכוּתָא 2, 37 + 18 times (in 7, 24 Ginsb. gives a var. מלכותה); מַלְכְּתָא 5, 10; *מִלְּתָא 2, 8 + 11 times; מָרָדְתָּא Ez. 4, 12; מַשְׁרוֹקִיתָא 3, 5. 7. 10. 15; נֶבְרַשְׁתָּא 5, 5; נִפְקְתָא Ez. 6, 4. 8; נִצְבְּתָא 2, 41; עֲבִידְתָּא 2, 49; Ez. 5, 8; קַדְמָיְתָא 7, 4; קִרְיְתָא Ez. 4, 12 + 5 times; רְבִיעָיְתָא 7, 19. 23; רְבוּתָא 5, 18. 19; 7, 27; רַבְּתָא 4, 27; שָׂהֲדוּתָא Gen. 31, 47; שְׁאֵלְתָא 4, 14; *שַׁעְתָּא 3, 6. 15; 4, 30 (in 3, 6 Ginsb. gives a var. שַׁעְתָּה).

Feminine nouns in the emphatic state singular are found with ה only in the following: *מַלְכוּתָה 2, 44 (here Ginsb. gives a var. מלכותא); *מִלְּתָה 2, 5; *שַׁעֲתָה 5, 5 (here Ginsb. gives a var. שעתא).

Feminine nouns in the emphatic plural are found with א as follows: אֶצְבְּעָתָא 2, 41; אַרְיָוָתָא 6, 8. 13. 17. 20. 21. 23. 25 (twice). 28; חֵיוָתָא 7, 7. 12. 19; מְדִינָתָא 3, 2. 3; מַלְכְוָתָא 2, 44; 7, 23; מְסַתְּרָתָא 2, 22; עֲמִיקָתָא 2, 22; פַּחֲוָתָא 3, 2. 3. 27; 6, 8; קַדְמָיָתָא 7, 8.

b) Feminine nouns in the absolute singular are found with א as follows: בְּטֵלָא Ez. 4, 24; חטיא (k) Ez. 6, 17; *חֵיוָא 4, 13 (Strack gives a var. חיוה); חֲמָא 3, 13 (Ginsb. gives a var. חמה); חֱמָא 3, 19; יְדָא 5, 5. 24; יַצִּיבָא 3, 24; 6, 13; 7, 16 (in the last place used adverbially, so also in 3, 24, although מִלְּתָא may be understood); *יַתִּירָא 6, 4 (Ginsb. gives a var. יתירה); מָרָדָא Ez. 4, 15; מִשְׁנֵיָא 7, 7; מִתְיַהֲבָא Ez. 6, 8; מִתְעַבְדָא Ez. 5, 8; עָבְדָא 7, 21; *קִרְיָא Ez. 4, 15; רביעיא (k) 2, 40; 3, 25; 7, 7. 23; שַׂבְּכָא 3, 5. 7. 10. 15; שִׁנְיָא 7, 5. 19; תְּדִירָא 6, 17. 21; תליתיא (k) 2, 39; *תַּקִּיפָא 7, 7.

Feminine nouns occur with ה as follows: אִגְּרָה Ez. 4, 8 (Ginsb. gives a var. אגרא); אָכְלָה 7, 7. 19; אַרְבְּעָה 3, 25; 7, 6. 17; אַרְכָה 4, 24 (Ginsb. gives a var. ארכא); 7, 12; בִּינָה 2, 21; גֵּוָה 4, 34; דְּחִילָה 7, 7. 19; דָּמְיָה 7, 5; זְעֵירָה 7, 8; חֲבוּלָה 6, 23 (Ginsb. gives a var. חבולא); חֲדָה 2, 9 + 8 times (in Ez. 4, 8 Ginsb. and in Dan. 2, 35 Strack give as a var. חדא); חֶדְוָה Ez. 6, 16; חַטָּאָה (k) Ez. 6, 17; *חֵיוָה 7, 5. 7; חָכְמָה 2, 30; 5, 11. 14; יָכְלָה 7, 21; יַקִּירָה 2, 11; *יַתִּירָה 3, 22 + 5 times (used adverbially in 7, 7. 19; Baer has יַתִּירָה everywhere except in 6, 4, where he gives יתירא; Strack cites certain MSS. which always have יתירא); כְּדָבָה 2, 9; כְּתָבָה 5, 5 (Ginsb. gives a var. כתבא); מְאָה 6, 2; Ez. 6, 17; 7, 22; מְגִלָּה Ez. 6, 2; מַדְּקָה 7, 7. 19; מְהַחְצְפָה 2, 15; מַחְצְפָה 3, 22; מִלָּה 2, 9. 10; מִנְדָּה Ez. 4, 13. 20; 7, 24; מִנְחָה 2, 46; מִתְנַשְּׂאָה Ez. 4, 19; נְבִזְבָּה 2, 6; סוּמְפֹּנְיָה 3, 5. 15; סיפניה (k) 3, 10 (Ginsb. gives a var. סיפניא); עַשְׂרָה 7, 24; עִלָּה 6, 5 (twice). 6; פֶּחָה Ez. 5, 14; פְּלִיגָה 2, 41; צִדְקָה 4, 24; קַיָּמָה 4, 23 (Ginsb. gives קימה only as a variant for קימא; Baer and Strack give קימה in the text and קימא as a variant); *קִרְיְתָה Ez. 4, 10; רָפְסָה 7, 7. 19; שִׁבְעָה 3, 19 + 4 times; שְׁחִיתָה 2, 9; 6, 5 (twice); מִשְׁנְיָה 7, 7 (Ginsb. gives a var. משניא); שָׁעָה 4, 16; תְּבִירָה 2, 42; תִּנְיָנָה 7, 5; *תַּקִּיפָה 2, 40. 42 (in 2, 42 Ginsb. gives a var. תקיפא).

c) Infinitives with א are found in *הוֹבָדָא (Strack gives הובדה) 2, 12. 24; בַּטָּלָא Ez. 4, 21 (Ginsb. gives a var. בַּטָּלָה); 6, 8; יַצָּבָא 7, 19.

Infinitives with ה are found as follows: *הוֹבָדָה 7, 26; הַיְתָיָה 3, 13; 5, 2; הִתְבְּהָלָה 2, 25; 3, 24; 6, 20; מִבְנְיָה Ez. 7, 15; הֲזָדָה 5,

20; חַבָלָה Ez. 6, 12; הַחֲוָיָה 2, 10. 16. 27; 3, 32; 5, 15 (in 2, 10 Ginsb. gives a var. הַחֲוָיָא); הֵיבָלָה Ez. 7, 15; הוֹדָעָה 5, 8; שַׁכְלָלָה Ez. 5, 3. 9; כַּפָּתָה 3, 20; נַסָּכָה 2, 46; הַנְסָקָה 6, 24; הַצָּלָה 3, 29; הַעֲלָה 5, 7; הַנְעָלָה 4, 3; קַטָּלָה 2, 14; הִתְקְטָלָה 2, 13; קַיָּמָה 6, 8; הַשְׁכָּחָה 6, 5 (twice); הַשְׁמָדָה 7, 26; הַשְׁנָיָה 6, 9. 16; 7, 25; Ez. 6, 12 (in the last passage Ginsb. gives a var. השניא); הַשְׁפָּלָה 4, 34; תַּקָּפָה 6, 8.

d) The pronoun אֲנַחְנָא occurs only in 3, 16. 17; Ez. 5, 11 (here Ginsb. gives a var. אנחנה); while אֲנַחְנָה is found in Ez. 4, 16. אנתה appears as k in 2, 29 + 14 times; אֲנָה occurs 13 times and אנא never (in 2, 8 and Ez. 6, 12 Ginsb. gives a var. אנא); דְּנָה also is uniform, being found 23 times in Ezra, 31 in Daniel and once in Jer. 10, 11 (in 2, 18 Ginsb. gives a var. דנא).

e) ה is found in the 2d pers. masc. sing. in חֲזַיְתָה 2, 41 (twice). 42; on the other hand א appears in תְּקִלְתָּא 5, 27 (Strack gives a var. תקלתה). Elsewhere the otiose letter is missing.

f) Verbs ל״א (ל״י) are found ending in א as follows: Perfect—*אֲתָא Ez. 5, 16; בְּעָא 2, 49; *הֲוָא 5, 19 + 5 times (in 6, 4 Ginsb. and Strack give a var. הוה); *מְטָא 4, 25; נְשָׂא 2, 35 (in שֵׁיצִיא Ez. 6, 15 the א is otiose). Imperfect—יִתְבְּנֵא Ez. 5, 15; 6, 3; תִּתְבְּנֵא Ez. 4, 13. 16. 21 (in Ez. 4, 16 Ginsb. gives a var. תתבנה); יִבְעֵא 6, 8, 13; אֶבְעֵא 7, 16; *לֶהֱוֵא 2, 28 + 15 times; *תֶּהֱוֵא 2, 40 + 3 times; אֲחַוֵּא 2, 24 (Baer has אֲחַוֵּה; Strack and Ginsb. give variants אֲחַוֵּה and אֲחַוֵּה); נְחַוֵּא 2, 4 (so Strack; Baer and Ginsb. have נְחַוֵּה); יְמַחֵא 4, 32; יִתְמְחֵא Ez. 6, 11; יִמְטֵא 4, 8. 17; תֶּעְדֵּא 6, 9. 13 (in both cases Ginsb. gives a var. תעדה, while Baer has תֶּעְדֵּה in the text); יִצְבֵּא 4, 14. 22. 29; תִּקְנֵא Ez. 7, 17; אֶקְרֵא 5, 17 (Strack gives a var. אקרה); יִתְרְמֵא 3, 6. 11; 6, 8. 13; יִשְׂגֵּא 3, 31; 6, 26; Ez. 4, 22; יִשְׁנֵא 7, 24; תִּשְׁנֵא 6, 8; 7, 23; יִשְׁתַּנֵּא 2, 9; יְהַשְׁנֵא Ez. 6, 11. Imperative—שֵׂא Ez. 5, 15. Participle—*בָּעֵא 6, 14; *גָּלֵא 2, 22. 28. 29; מַחֵא 5, 19; מְהוֹדֵא 2, 23; מוֹדֵא 6, 11; מְנֵא 5, 25 (twice). 26; צָבֵא 5, 19; מְצַלֵּא 6, 11; קָרֵא 3, 4; 4, 11; 5, 7; מְהַשְׁנֵא 2, 21; שָׁרֵא 2, 22; מְשָׁרֵא 5, 12. Infinitive—מֵזֵא 3, 19; מֵתֵא 3, 2; מִבְנֵא Ez. 5, 2. 17; 6, 8; לִבְנֵא Ez. 5, 3. 13; מִבְעֵא 2, 18; מִגְלֵא 2, 47; מֶחֱזֵא Ez. 4, 14; מִקְרֵא 5, 8. 16; מִרְמֵא 3, 20; מִשְׁרֵא 5, 16.

Verbs ל״א (ל״י) are found with final ה as follows: Perfect—*אֲתָה 7, 22; Ez. 5, 3; *בְּעָה 2, 16 (Baer בעא); *הֲוָה 4, 26 + 6 times; חֲזָה 4, 20; 7, 1 (in 4, 20 Ginsb. gives a var. חזא); *מְטָה 7, 13. 22; מְנָה 5, 26; רְבָה 4, 8. 17. 30. Imperfect—*לֶהֱוֵה 4, 22; *תֶּהֱוֵה 2,

41. 42; 4, 24; יְהֶהֱוֵה 5, 12; נֶהֱוֵה 2, 7; יַעְדֵּה 7, 14; יִקְרֵה 5, 7; יִשְׁתַּוֵּה 3, 29. Participles—אָתֵה 7, 13; אֵזֵה 3, 22; *בָּעֵה 6, 12; *גָּלֵה 2, 47; דָּמֵה 3, 25; חָזֵה 2, 31+14 times; חֲזֵה 3, 19; מְהַעְדֵּה 2, 21 (Ginsb. gives a var. מהעדא); עָנֵה 2, 5+21 times; שְׁלֵה 4, 1; שָׁתֵה 5, 1.

7. A similar fluctuation appears in the early Aramaic inscriptions, so much so that Lidzbarski remarks (p. 20): "In verbs third ה (א) and in the *st. abs. fem. sing.* as well as the *st. emph.* the use of ה and א fluctuates down to the latest times, but the oldest texts show a preference for ה." Examples are as follows (as noted above, references, unless otherwise specified, are to the *CIS.*; for abbreviations see Lidzbarski, pp. 4, 507):

a) In the masc. sing. emph. st., ה occurs for א only in זנה (דנה) (BA דְּנָה) and in the following forms, which, however, are not entirely certain: אבנה proper name 122, 1. 2; חקלה 53, 1 (also חקלא, e. g., 113, 18: Syr. ܚܩܠܐ): כרמה Si., Eut. 99, 2 (Syr. ܟܪܡܐ); קישה name of a deity (cf. Baethgen, *Beiträge z. semit. Religionsgeschichte*, 1888, 108) Na., 197, 5; 198, 4 (also קישא Na., 209, 9); שאה (*grain?*) Pan. 6, 9. In the fem. emph. st. ה appears only in the doubtful form נפקתה (which could be taken as with suff. 3 sing.; BA נפקתא, Syr. ܢܦܩܬܐ) 146 A, 1. In Christian Palestinian final ā is represented by ה instead of א only in a few evidently uncertain cases, viz. ܚܝܝܗ ܕܠܥܠܡ, *eternal life*, John 5, 24 (elsewhere always ܚܝܝܐ), and ܐܪܟܘܢܝܗ ܕܥܡܗ, *the rulers of the people*, Luke 24, 20; cf. Nöldeke, *ZDMG.*, 22 (1868), 448 (the forms may, of course, be taken as with suffix 3 sing., after the type ܣܝܡܝܗ ܕܡܠܟܬܐ, Nöldeke, § 205, C).

b) In the feminine ending of nouns ה appears as follows: אמה Na. proper name 204, 2; 271, 3 (Eut. 18, 1?); חדה Had. 28; Na., 218, 4; 221, 6 (also חדא Pa., T II b, 10; BA חֲדָה, Syr. ܚܕܐ); חטה Pan., 6. 9 (also חטא Pa., T II b, 9 = Arab. حِنْطَة); חטיאה Na., 224, 11 (= Arab. خَطِيئَة to which Syr. (ܐ)ܚܛܝܬܐ—by analogy—corresponds); מוהבה Na., 209, 6; 219, 5 (= Arabic مَوْهَبَة); מאה Na., 205, 9; Si., Eut. 457, 1 (BA מְאָה, Syr. ܡܐܐ); cf. תלתמאה Pa., Vog. 6, 4, and חמשמאה Na., 200, 9; צדקה 145 A, 5 (BA צִדְקָה, Syr. ܙܕܩܬܐ); שנה 113, 20 (Syr. ܫܢܬܐ); שורה and שערה Pan. 6. 9 (cf. Cooke, p. 176); also in the following participles, פלחה 141, 3; בריכה 141, 1. 3; Si., Eut. 393; 394, 1.

c) No instance occurs with ה in the ending of infinitives.

d) In verbs ל״א (ל״י): Perfect—אתה Zenj. C, 2 (Lidzb., p. 444)?; בנה Na., 162; 163, C; 164, 3; 182, 1, also in the Na. proper name בנהבל 158, 5; הוה Na., 224, 4; ענה 145 B, 2; Pa., Vog. 83 b, 3; 105, 3. Imperfect—תהוה Pa., T II c, 28; יהוה 149 B C (uncertain); ישרה 145 A, 7. Participles—חזה (act.) Ner. 2, 5; מתקרה Pa., Vog. 34, 6; Chediac 1, 5 (also מתקרא Na., 158, 2 and elsewhere); משרה line 2 of the hunting inscription in Cilicia (Lidzb., p. 446; Cooke, No. 68).

8. Thus it will be seen that, while in Syriac feminine nouns as well as masculine nouns in the emphatic state regularly end in א (Nöldeke, § 70; Brockelmann, §§ 98, 99), in BA, on the other hand, feminine nouns in a majority of cases end in ה,[a] while the emphatic state usually has א.[b]

[a] In Arabic it is the rule that feminine nouns with the formative suffix *-at* should be written with ة in the absolute and construct states, as, e. g., مَدِينَةٌ and مَدِينَةُ ٱلنَّبِيِّ. The orthographic principle underlying this method is, as Nöldeke (*Beiträge zur semitischen Sprachwissenschaft*, 1904, 7) tells us, that in Arabic the consonants are written as the words were spoken when isolated, each by itself, i. e., unconnected with the preceding word, and in the pausal form with reference to the following word. Now, the pausal form (وَقْفٌ) of the feminine ends in *-ah* (for *-at*), the *h* being sounded, and not otiose (Vernier, I, 115; see Wright, I, 7 footnote, 184A). In Hebrew and Aramaic the absolute state of nouns is properly a pausal form (see Margolis, *AJSL.*, XII (1896), 203). Hence the spelling with ה in BA, referred to in the text, agrees with the history of the form; in other words, the orthography here is historical. Where feminine nouns are written in BA with א at the end, the historical orthography is given up in favor of phonetic spelling under the analogical influence, it would appear, of the emphatic state (see under [b]); in Syriac the analogy is there regular.

[b] One of the theories as to the origin of the emphatic state in Aramaic is that it is a development from the old Semitic accusative (cf. Barth, *AJSL.*, 1901, 50). If this be so, א corresponds to the ا in the pausal form in Arabic (Vernier, I, 113). Thus: مَلِكًا, pause مَلِكَا = מַלְכָּא. The use of ה in certain instances may be due to analogy with the feminine (see under [a]).

9. In BA, as in Hebrew, ה is used in the prefix of the perfect, imperfect, and infinitive of the causative stem (add the

examples of the imperfect and participle with ה not syncopated, given below, § 26, and the participle of the Hoph'al, given in § 48), as well as in the prefix of the perfect and infinitive of the passive (reflexive) stems, א appearing only occasionally. This is regarded by Kautzsch as an Hebraism (*GBA.*, § 23, 1, rem. 1).

The examples with הַ are as follows: Haph'el perfect: 3d sing. masc. הֵימִן 6, 24; הַיְתִי 5, 13; הַגְלִי Ez. 4, 10; 5, 12; הֵיבֵל Ez. 5, 14; 6, 5; הוֹדַע 2, 15. 17. 28. 45; הוֹדְעָךְ 2, 29; הוֹתֵב Ez. 4, 10; הַנְפֵּק 5, 2; Ez. 5, 14 (twice); 6, 5; הַנְעֵל 2, 25; 6, 19; הַצְלַח 3, 30; 6, 29; הֲקִים 3, 2. 3. 5; הֲקִים 6, 2; *הֲקִימֵהּ 5, 11; הַשְׁלְטֵהּ 2, 48; הַשְׁלְטָךְ 2, 38; הַשְׁלְמֵהּ 5, 26; הֲתִיב 2, 14; 3d fem. sing. הַדֶּקֶת 2, 34. 45; הֶקְמַת 7, 5; 2d masc. sing. הוֹדַעְתַּנִי 2, 23; הוֹדַעְתֶּנָא 2, 23; הֲקִימְתָּ 3, 12. 18; הַשְׁפֵּלְתְּ 5, 22; 1st sing. הֲקֵימֶת 3, 14; הַשְׁכַּחַת 2, 25; 3d plural, הַיְתִיו 5, 3. 23; 6, 17. 25; הַדִּקוּ 6, 25; הֶחֱסִנוּ 7, 22; הַכְרִזוּ 5, 29; הַלְבִּשׁוּ 5, 29; הַנְפִּקוּ 5, 3; הַסִּקוּ 3, 22; הֶעְדִּיו 5, 20; 7, 12; הֲקִימוּ Ez. 6, 18; הַקְרִבוּ Ez. 6, 17; הַקְרְבוּהִי 7, 13; הַרְגִּזוּ Ez. 5, 12; הַרְגִּשׁוּ 6, 7. 12. 16; הַשְׁכַּחוּ 6, 12; Ez. 4, 19; הֲתִיבוּנָא Ez. 5, 11; 1st plural, הוֹדַעְנָא Ez. 4, 14; הַשְׁכַּחְנָא 6, 6; imperative הַעֵלְנִי 2, 24; הַשְׁלֵם Ez. 7, 19; הַחֲוֹנִי 2, 6. Hithpe'el perfect: 3d masc. sing. הִשְׁתְּכַח 2, 35; 6, 24; Ez. 6, 2; הִתְמְלִי 3, 19; 3d fem. sing. *הִתְגְּזֶרֶת 2, 34; הִשְׁתְּכַחַת 5, 11. 12. 14; 6, 5. 23; 2d masc. sing. הִשְׁתְּכַחַתְּ 5, 27: 3d plural, הִתְרְחִצוּ 3, 28. Hithpa'el perfect, 3d masc. sing. הִתְהָרָךְ 3, 27; הִתְנַבִּי Ez. 5, 1; 3d plural, הִתְנַדַּבוּ Ez. 7, 15; 2d plural, הִזְדְּמִנְתּוּן (k) 2, 9. Hithpo'lal perfect, 2d masc. sing. הִתְרוֹמַמְתָּ 5, 23. To the infinitives given above (§ 6) add the following: הוֹדָעֻתָךְ Ez. 5, 10; הוֹדָעֻתַנִי 2, 26; 4, 15; 5, 15. 16; הַנְזָקַת Ez. 4, 22; הַצְלָוּתֵהּ 6, 15; הֲקָמוּתֵהּ 6, 4; הֲתָבוּתָךְ 3, 16; הִתְנַדָּבוּת Ez. 7, 16.

Following are the examples with א: Haph'el perfect, *אֲקִימֵהּ 3, 1; imperative, אַחֵת Ez. 5, 15; אַתַּרוּ 4, 11; infinitive, אֲהָיָית 5, 12. Hithpe'el, *אִתְגְּזֶרֶת 2, 45; אִתְכְּרִיַּת 7, 15; אתעקרו (k), אִתְעֲקַרָה (k), 7, 8. Hithpa'al, אשתנו (k), אִשְׁתַּנִּי 3, 19; אִתְיָעַטוּ 6, 8. Ethpo'lal, אֶשְׁתּוֹמַם 4, 16.

10. In the inscriptions a similar fluctuation appears in the use of ה and א, the older inscriptions having more frequently ה. Following are the examples taken from Lidzbarski:

With הַ. Haph'el, 3d masc. sing. הארך Ner. 2, 3; הכבר Pan. 4; העבר Pan. 18; הקם Pan. 18; *הקים Na., 161, I, 1; הקרב 75, 4;

הרפי Pan. 7 (twice); השחת Had. 29; with suff. 3d sing. masc. היטיבה. Pan. 9; with suff. 1st sing. הושבני Pan. 19; Bauin. 5; 1st sing. הושבת Had. 19; הקמת Had. 1; with suff. 3d sing. masc. היטבתה Bauin. 12; Hithnaph'al (root אבה or יאב, cf. Lidzbarski, 205) התנאבו Bauin. 14.

With א. 'Aph'el, אתי (for אאתי, cf. Arabic آتَى) Pa., Vog. 15, 4; איתי in the proper name איתיבל 196, 3; אחבר Pa., Nöldeke 2; אחיי Na., 183, 3; אפק Pa., T. II b, 43; אסק Pa., Vog. 3, 1; *אקים Pa., Vog. 13, 2; B 1, 3; Vog. 4, 3; Eut. 103, 2; אשר (rt. שרר) Pa., T. II c, 21; 3d fem. sing. אקימת Pa., Vog. 7, 3; 11, 2; אשרת Pa., T. I, 3; 1st sing. אקימת Pa., T. II c, 10; with suff. 3d masc. sing. אחברתה Pa., Nöldeke 6; 3d pl. אקימו Na., 164, 1; Vog. 5, 3 (B 2, 3); אחרבו Si., Eut. 463, 3; אסקו Pa., T. I, 5; infinitive, אחבורא Pa., Vog. 71; Ethpa'al, perfect 3d sing. fem. אשלמת (with ש doubled for אשתלמת) Pa., Vog. 95, 4.

11. While in Arabic the usual preformative of the IV is أ there are certain rare forms with ه, as هَرَاحَ for أَرَاحَ, هَرَادَ for أَرَادَ, هَرَاقَ for أَرَاقَ (Heb. הֵרִיק), هَنَارَ for أَنَارَ, هَاتَ for آتَ (root أَتَى, Aramaic אֲתָה), هَنْدَسَ, هَيْمَنَ (Heb. הֶאֱמִין), Wright, *Arab. Gram.*, I, § 45, rem. d. With reference to the last example it must be said that it is a loan-word ultimately from the Hebrew; cf. Syriac ܗܝܡܢ (Nöldeke, *Mand.*, § 163). In the Sabæan dialect ה regularly occurs as the preformative, whereas in the corresponding Minæan dialect ש is employed, ההדתו, etc. (Hommel, *Süd-arab. Chrestomathie*, 1893, § 23). In Mandaic also ה is found occasionally, e. g., האוליל (Syr. ܐܝܠܠ, Heb. הֵילִיל), האנפיק (also אפיק), האנסיק (also אסיק); as a loan-word (see above) האימאן; cf. also the inf. האנדוזיא (by the side of the *nomen actionis* אנדאזתא); cf. Arabic هَنْدَسَ (Nöldeke, *Mand.*, § 163).

Thus, although BA and Hebrew agree in the use of ה in the preformative of the Haph'el (Hiph'il), in view of the fact that ה is found in the inscriptions and in Sabæan, and sporadically in Arabic and Mandaic, we need not assume Hebrew influence to account for its use in BA.

12. The following words are written in BA with שׁ:

בְּשַׂר (Syr. ܒܣܪ) 7, 5: בִּשְׂרָא 2, 11; 4, 9; נְשָׂא 2, 35; שֵׂא Ez. 5, 15; מִתְנַשְּׂאָה Ez. 4, 19; עֲשַׂב (Syr. ܥܣܒ) 4, 12; עִשְׂבָּא 4, 22. 29. 30; 5, 21; עֲשַׂר (Syr. ܥܣܪ) 4, 26; 7, 7. 20. 24; Ez. 6, 17; עַשְׂרָה 7, 24; עֶשְׂרִין 6, 2; שָׂבֵי (Syr. ܣܐܒ) Ez. 5, 5; 6, 7. 8. 14; שָׂבַיָּא Ez. 5, 9; יִשְׂגֵּא (root שגא, Syr. ܣܓܐ) 3, 31; 6, 26; Ez. 4, 22; שַׂגִּיא 2, 6 + 10 times; שַׂגִּיאָן 2, 48; Ez. 5. 11; שָׂהֲדוּתָא (Syr. ܣܗܕܘܬܐ) Gen. 31, 47; שָׂמְתָּ (root שום, Syr. ܣܘܡ) 3, 10; שָׂמֶת Ez. 6, 12; שָׂם Ez. 5, 3 + 7 times; שָׂמֵהּ Ez. 5, 14; שָׂמוּ 3, 12; שִׂימוּ Ez. 4, 21; שִׂים 3, 29 + 6 times; שָׂמַת 6, 18; יִתְּשָׂם Ez. 4, 21; יִתְּשָׂמוּן 2, 5; מִתְּשָׂם Ez. 5, 8; שְׂטַר (Syr. ܣܛܪܐ) 7, 5; שָׂכְלְתָנוּ 5, 11. 12. 14; מִשְׂתַּכַּל 7, 8; שָׂנְאָ (Syr. ܣܢܐ) 4, 16; שְׂעַר (Syr. ܣܥܪ) 3, 27; 7, 9: שְׂעַרֵהּ 4, 30; also שַׂבְּכָא (Greek σαμβύκη) 3, 5. 7. 10. 15 (in 3, 5 Ginsb. gives a var. סבכא); and the following proper names: אַרְתַּחְשַׁשְׂתָּא Ez. 4, 7 (twice). 8. 11. 23; 7, 15; cf. אַרְתַּחְשַׁסְתָּא Ez. 7, 12. 21; יִשְׂרָאֵל (Syr. ܝܣܪܝܠ Matt. 2, 6) Ez. 6, 14 + 5 times; כַּשְׂדָּי 2, 10; כַּשְׂדָּיֵא (k) 2, 5; 4, 4; 5, 7, 30; כַּשְׂדָּאִין 3, 8.

Kautzsch, though referring to certain instances where שׂ is used in the inscriptions, regards the use of שׂ in BA as an Hebraism.

13. There seem to have been originally three sibilants in Semitic, the exact pronunciation of which cannot now be determined. They were not, however, given a uniform pronunciation throughout the Semitic area. There existed dialectic variations; cf. Judges 12, 6 for an instance among the Hebrews. This irregularity in pronunciation explains the absence of a fixed method for distinguishing the sibilants in writing. Only with the growth of a literature was the usage crystallized, one custom coming to be regarded as the standard. The BA dates from the period of uncertainty, and the promiscuous use of שׂ and ס, so far from being due to Hebrew influence, is rather an evidence of conformity to the usage of early Aramaic. The inscriptions, especially the earlier ones, show a similar irregularity in writing the sibilants.

Thus: עשתור Pa. proper name, Vog. 4, 2 (Cooke, 113, 2) transcribed Ασθώρου; cf. עסתורגא Pa. proper name, Müller, 46, 2

(Cooke, 143, 2), and עבד־עסתור, Scheil, 2, 1; 3, 1; פרש, *CIS.*, II, 10, explained in the Assyrian section as meaning "a half mina;" cf. פרס Pan. 6; cf. also Dan. 5, 25 (cf. Bevan, p. 106). שגיאן "great," Pa., Vog., 15, 5 (Cooke, 121, 5); cf. סגיאן in the same line and שגין Pa., T. I, 6; שמאל Bauin. 2 f., 17; *Sam'al* name of a country, perhaps = Hebrew שְׂמֹאל "the left," i. e., "the north;" cf. Pa. סמלך "thy left hand," Nöldeke, *ZA.*, 14 (1894), 264–267; שריכו proper name transcribed σοραιχον (= Arab. شَرِيك) Vog. 11, 1; 12, 1; Afr. 1, 2; also probably 13, 2; cf. סריכו Vog. 26, 4; 101, 3. Lidzbarski (p. 372) mentions also שבע "to satisfy" and refers to Cl. Ganneau's Pa. I, 7, also שבען proper name 115.

The inscriptions seem to be irregular also in their transcription of the sibilants in Assyrian and Babylonian proper names (Lidzbarski, p. 392). Thus:

Assyrian s = ש, in חבשו, נשך, שנזרבן, שנסרצר, שרכן
" s = ס, in אתרמסין, סנצר
" $\check{s}$ = ס, in אסר, ארבלסר, סג, סר, תגלתפליסר
" $\check{s}$ elsewhere = ש
Babylonian s = ס, in מרסגלמר.

14. The traditional[a] pronunciation of Hebrew שׁ and the uncertainty of orthography which permits שׂ and ס to be used promiscuously for each other[b] notwithstanding, we possess sufficient evidence that originally שׂ and ס represented distinct sounds. The proof is, first, that in the South Arabic alphabet the sounds corresponding to the Hebrew שׁ, שׂ, and ס are represented by three distinct symbols, ᚢ, ≶, and ᛝ;[c] secondly, that the graphic differentiation of שׁ and שׂ by means of a diacritic point comes from late Masoretic times,[d] thus showing that in an older period the two sounds for which the symbol ש was used were nearer to each other than either was to ס. The consensus of opinion among scholars is that primitive Semitic possessed three s-sounds, the exact pronunciation of which cannot now be determined, and which, although more or less similar, were sufficiently distinct to warrant the creation of three distinct symbols in Southern Arabic. The following table shows these three s-sounds and their permutations in the various Semitic dialects:

Ass.	Aram.	Heb.	Arab.	Sabæan	Ethiopic
s	ס	ס	[س]	𐩯	ሰ
$\check{s}_1$[f]	▲	שׂ	س	𐩪	ሰ
$\check{s}_2$[f]	[ס]	שׁ	ش	𐩦	ሠ

[a] We are in the habit of pronouncing שׁ *š* like English *sh* and שׂ like English *s*. However, among certain sections of the Jews the pronunciation is just the reverse. Cf. Schreiner, "Zur Gesch. der Aussprache des Hebräischen," *ZAW.*, VI (1886), 258, 3; D. H. Müller, "Zur Gesch. der semitischen Zischlaute," *Intern. Congr. of Orientalists*, VII (Vienna, 1889), 233, 2; Lagarde, *Mitt.*, IV (1891), 374 ff.; Lambert, *REJ.*, XLIX (1904), 146 f.

[b] אכלה ואכלה, ed. Frensdorff, 1864, No. 191, contains a list of eighteen words with שׂ in the place of ס: On the other hand, we sometimes find ס for שׁ = Arabic ش; e. g., סְתָו Cant. 2, 11 = Arabic شتاء (Hommel, *Aufsätze und Abhandlungen*, I [1892], 105).

[c] Cf. Hommel, *op. cit.*, 104; "Das Samech in den minäo-sabäischen Inschriften," *ZDMG.*, XLVI (1892), 528–538; *Süd-arabische Chrestomathie*, 1893, § 12.

[d] Cf. Haupt, *ZDMG.*, XXXIV (1886), 763 (under the date of November, 1879): "The Hebrew שׂ I regard only as a product of the authors of the punctuation. Thus, e. g., there can be no doubt that כַּשְׂדִּים was originally pronounced *kašdim*, although the *š* may have been different from that in שׁוֹר 'ox' and in שֵׁם 'name.' Subsequently this *š* came to be sounded like *s*, as in Ass., Eth., and Aram. The punctators accordingly marked the ש in those words in which it was pronounced ס with the point on the left, and the ש which even in later times continued to be pronounced as *š*, with the point on the right." Similarly Stade, *Gramm.*, 1879, § 68 *b*; König, *Lehrgebäude*, I, 1881, 35.

[e] Haupt, *loc. cit.*, 762: "ס appears in all Semitic languages as ס, and therefore may be supposed to have existed as ס in primitive Semitic; ▲, on the other hand, appears in Ass., Heb., and Aram. as *š*, in Eth. and Arabic, however, as *s*. I believe that here the Eth. and Arabic approach the phonetic conditions of primitive Semitic most closely. In primitive Semitic ▲ represented an *s* which originally was distinct from the *s* which appears in Hebrew as ס; in Eth. and Arabic, however, they became identified, while in Ass., Heb., and Aram. the first *s*-sound came to be pronounced *š*. As for ش, it appears in Ass., Eth., and Arabic as *š*—which probably was also its original pronunciation—while in Hebrew it is found as שׁ and in Aram. as ס. In Ass. and Eth. likewise this *š* in course of time became *s*." D. H. Müller, *loc. cit.*, 246: "The original Semitic possessed three sibilants, the exact pronunciation of which cannot now

be determined. We will represent them by *š*, *s*, and *ś* (i. e., שׁ, שׂ, ס). Of these three consonants *š* and *s* stand closer to each other than either does to *ś*." Cf. also Zimmern, 11; 14 f.; Lindberg, 73 f.

[f] Cf. Delitzsch, *Assyrian Grammar*, § 46.

15. The absence of a special symbol in Syriac for the sound represented in BA by שׂ as little disproves the existence of such a sound in Aramaic as the absence of a symbol in Arabic for 𐩯 proves that the sound was originally wanting in Arabic. The truth is that both in Hebrew and in Aramaic the שׂ sound, originally nearer to שׁ than to ס, in course of time came to be sounded like ס. The Masoretes, both in the Hebrew and Aramaic texts of the Bible, endeavored, as a rule, to retain the historical spelling with ש, preferring to indicate the modern pronunciation by a diacritic point. In Syriac the identification of the שׂ and ס sounds led to the phonetic spelling with ܣ uniformly. The use of שׂ for ܣ in BA, in view of the orthography of early Aramaic inscriptions, as well as of the considerations derived from a comparison with the other Semitic languages, can by no means be considered a Hebraism, but is rather a part of early Aramaic orthography. Of course, the diacritic point indicating the ס pronunciation of one of the two cognate sounds represented by ש is a Masoretic device common to the Hebrew and Aramaic portions of the Old Testament.

[a] Cf. Nöldeke (he is treating of the Palmyrene inscriptions), *ZDMG.*, XXIV (1870), 95: "As far as the sibilants are concerned, we find ש several times where we should expect to find ס; thus in שגיאן, ערשא and שרן. In all these cases Hebrew has שׂ and we must read שׂ. However, I regard this manner of writing only as a reminiscence of an older form of language, because the fact that the specific consonant שׂ (differing as well from שׁ as from ס) does not occur elsewhere, but, as usual in Aramaic, had become ס, is proved by the use of סגיאן in close proximity to שגיאן and by סהד 'to witness,' which etymologically should also have שׂ."

16. The doubling of a consonant in BA, as in Hebrew, is organic in the Pa'el (Pi'el); e. g., תְּקַבְּלוּן 2, 6, etc.; and the Hithpa'al (Hithpa'el); e. g., תִּתְחַבַּל 2, 44, etc. This, of course, is a part of general Semitic grammar. The intensified meaning is expressed by an increase of volume within the stem

(Stade, § 154 *a;* König, II, 379). In Syriac, with regard to doubling in general, it must be remarked that only the Eastern Syrians continued to pay attention to it, while the Western Syrians gave it up at a very early date. The vocalization, however, unmistakably points to the general prevalence of doubling in the earlier stages of Aramaic; in other words, BA is proved to be more primitive than Syriac in this respect.

17. Equally a common Semitic feature is the doubling of the middle (forms faʻʻal, faʻʻil, etc.; Kautzsch, § 59; Barth, *Nomen.* xi) or third (forms fiʻill, fuʻull; so at least according to Barth, §§ 95 ff.; usually the doubling in these forms is regarded as artificial; see below 24) radical in certain formations expressing intensity, although not derived from the so-called Intensive stem.

18. Assimilation of vowelless נ takes place in BA as in Hebrew (GK, § 19, 2 *a*):

a) With מִן, מִטַּל 4, 22. 30; 5. 21; מִטְּעֵם Ez. 6, 14; מִנִּכְסֵי Ez. 6, 8. In all other cases the נ is retained, not only before laryngeals, as מִן־אֱדַיִן (cf. Heb. מֵאָז) Ez. 5, 16; מִן־הֵיכְלָא 5, 2; Ez. 6, 5; מִן־חַבְרָתַהּ 7, 20; מִן־עָלְמָה (cf. Heb. מֵעוֹלָם) 2, 20; but also before other consonants, as מִן־בֵּית (Heb. מִבֵּית) Ez. 6, 5, etc.; מִן־גַּבָּא 6, 24, etc.; מִן־דָּא 7, 4; מִן־טַעַם Ez. 6, 14; מִן־יַד (מִיַּד) 6, 29; מִן־כָּל־ (Heb. מִכָּל־) 7, 7, etc.; מִן־מַלְכָּא (cf. Heb. מִמֶּלֶךְ) 2, 16, etc.; מִן־נִצְבְּתָא 2, 41; מִן־קֳאמַיָּא 7, 16; מִן־רִבּוּתָא 5, 19; מִן־שְׁמַיָּא (cf. Heb. מִשָּׁמַיִם) 4, 20, etc.; מִן־תְּחוֹת (cf. מִתַּחַת) Jer. 10, 11. It will thus be seen that the assimilation of the נ of מִן is rather rare in BA as compared with Hebrew, where the rule is that while the נ remains in the majority of cases before the article (i. e., before the laryngeal הַ) it is otherwise usually assimilated.

b) In verbs פ״ן, אחת (Syr. ܐܶܚܶܬ) Ez. 5, 15; תַּחֵת Ez. 6, 5; מְהַחֲתִין Ez. 6, 1; יִפֵּל (Syr. ܢܶܦܶܠ) 3, 6. 10. 11; תִּפְּלוּן 3, 15; הַצְלָה 3, 29; הַצָּלוּתֵהּ 6, 15; מַצִּל 6, 28; מַתְּנָן 2, 6. 48; מַתְּנָתָךְ 5, 17; אַתַּרוּ (Syr. ܐܰܬܰܪܘ) 4, 11.

19. נ remains unassimilated in BA:

a) As in Hebrew before laryngeals, הַנְחַת (cf. Heb. הַנְחַת Joel 4, 11) 5, 20; מִנְחָה Heb. מִנְחָה) 2, 46; שִׁלְטֹנֵיהוֹן 7, 12.

b) In verbs פ״ן, הַנְזָקַת Ez. 4, 22; מְהַנְזְקַת Ez. 4, 15; תְּהַנְזִק Ez. 4, 13; הַנְפֵּק (Syr. ܐܰܦܶܩ) 5, 2; Ez. 5, 14 (twice); 6, 5; הַנְפִּקוּ 5, 3; יִנְתֶּן־ (cf. Syr. ܢܶܬܶܠ) 2, 16; תִּנְתֵּן Ez. 7, 20; יִנְתְּנוּן Ez. 4, 13; לְמִנְתַּן Ez. 7, 20.

c) In roots ע״נ, אַנְפּוֹהִי (Syr. ܐܰܦܰܘܗܝ, Heb. אַפָּיו) 2, 46; 3, 19; always in the pronoun אנתה (k, i. e., אַנְתְּה, k אַנְתָּה, Syr. ܐܰܢ݇ܬ); בִּנְזַי (Syr. ܓܶܙܳܐ or ܓܶܙܳܐ contracted from ܓܶܢܙܳܐ) Ez. 7, 20 and בִּנְזַיָּא Ez. 5, 17; 6, 1; חִנְטִין (Syr. ܚܶܛܳܐ, Heb. חִטָּה) Ez. 6, 9; 7, 22; עַנְפּוֹהִי (cf. Syr. ܥܰܦܳܐ, Heb. עַנְפְּכֶם) 4, 9 + 5 times.

d) In the following examples: בִּנְיָנָא Ez. 5, 4; חֲנַנְיָה 2, 17; לְמִנְיַן Ez. 6, 17; תִּנְיָנָה (Syr. ܬܶܢܝܳܢܳܐ) 7, 5; תִּנְיָנוּת (Syr. ܬܢܝܳܢܽܘܬ) 2, 7; שׁוּשַׁנְכָיֵא Ez. 4, 9. In סוּמְפֹּנְיָה 3, 10, סֻמְפֹּנְיָה 3, 5. 15 and מְדִינְתָּא (Syr. ܡܕܺܝܢ݇ܬܳܐ) Ez. 5, 8; 6, 2, the ְ under נ represents a Greek or Semitic vowel lost in Aramaic. In פְּסַנְתֵּרִין 3, 5. 10. 15 and פְּסַנְטֵרִין 3, 7, the נ stands for *l* as shown by the Greek *ψαλτήριον*. (On the interchange of *n* and *l* cf. Haupt, *SBOT.*, Isaiah, p. 121, l. 48.)

e) As in Hebrew, after the non-formative (separable, representing an originally separate word in proclisis) prefixes ב and כ, in בִּנְבוּאַת Ez. 6, 14 and כִּנְמַר 7, 6.

20. On the whole, the same principles obtain in Syriac. As first radical, נ is almost always assimilated after a prefix; cf. ܐܰܦܶܩ for ܐܰܢܦܶܩ, ܡܰܦܩܳܐ for ܡܰܢܦܩܳܐ, etc. As second radical, נ is assimilated in certain nouns, as ܥܶܩܳܐ (for ܥܶܢܩܳܐ* cf. Heb. עֲנָק Cant. 4, 9 [Lagarde, *Übersicht*, 175: עֲנָק—form fiʿāl—to ܥܶܩܳܐ—form fiʿl—as חֲלוֹק to חֵלֶק, חֲלוֹם to BA חֵלֶם, ܣܶܬܪܳܐ to סֵתֶר, ܛܶܠܳܠܳܐ to צֵל, ܬܶܠܳܠܳܐ to תֵּל, ܬܶܠܳܐ]; cf. Margolis, *AJSL.*, XII (1896), 215), ܐܰܦܳܐ, etc., as compared with ܥܶܢܩܳܐ, etc. (it is immaterial, as far as Syriac is concerned, whether the syllable was originally closed in early Aramaic, or became closed in Syriac). The ܢ which is dropped in pronunciation is sometimes retained in writing, e. g., in ܢܶܢܣܰܒ (cf. ܢܶܣܰܒ), ܐܰܢ݇ܬܬܳܐ, ܐܰܢ݇ܬ, etc. Similarly, before ܬܳܐ, ܢ frequently loses its sound, at times even when retained in writing; e. g., ܓܶܦܬܳܐ (cf. Heb. גֶּפֶן), ܒܶܢ݇ܬܳܐ (cf. בְּבִינָה), ܠܒܶܢ݇ܬܳܐ (cf. Heb. לְבֵנָה), ܬܺܐܢ݇ܬܳܐ (cf. Heb. תאנה);

and ܡܕܝܢ̱ܬܳܐ (cf. מְדִינְתָּא), ܣܦܝܢ̱ܬܳܐ (cf. Heb. סְפִינָה), ܫܢ̱ܬܳܐ (cf. שַׁתָּא, Targum, שת Mesha stone, 2, 8, and elsewhere; see below, § 17).

21. In the early Aramaic inscriptions there is irregularity as to the assimilation or non-assimilation of נ. Sometimes the same word is written in both ways.

Following are the examples collected from Lidzbarski's glossary: יהחון (root נחת; observe that the נ is assimilated before ח as in Syriac and BA, 145 B, 6; יסחו (root נסח) Ner. 1, 9; ינסחוהי 113, 14; נפק, with assimilation always in the Palmyrene Tarif, as אפק II *b*, 43; מפק II *a*, 31; *b*, 31 ff.; מפקא II *b*, 47; מאפק II *c*, 12; מפקן II *b*, 16; מפקנא II *a*, 11 ff.; ממפקנא II *c*, 44; without assimilation, יהנפק 113, 21; ינפק Na. 197, 2; 198, 5. 9; 206, 5; 207, 3; מנצבא (root נצב) Pa., Müller, C, 1; inf. לנצב Had., 10 (twice); נצר always without assimilation, ינצר Ner. 1, 13; תנצר Ner. 1, 12 (in Hebrew this word is always יִצְּרוּ in non-pausal forms, cf. Prov. 20, 28, but יִנְצֹ֑רוּ when in pause, cf. Deut. 33, 9; GK, § 66, 2 Rem. 1. On לִנְצֹר Prov. 2, 8 cf. Haupt, *SBOT.*, p. 35, l. 30: "For the non-assimilation of the נ in לִנְצֹר cf. the Ass. Šaf'el ušanṣir [Del., *HW.*, 477 *b*; *Assyr. Gr.*, § 49 *b*]. In Assyrian antedental *n* is, as a rule, not assimilated in cases where the assimilation would produce ambiguity; e. g., *enzu* "goat" in distinction from *ezzu* "strong;" *enšu* "weak" in distinction from *eššu* (-*edšu*, *ḥadšu*) "new," etc.); יתן (root נתן) Had., 23; 149 BC, 12; Pa., T., II *a*, 5; *b*, 20; יתנו Had., 4; and the doubtful case (י)תנון 138 B, 2; cf. also ינתן 145 D, 1; Na. 197, 3. 6; 198. 5.

22. This irregularity is a mark of the growth of the language. It points back to a period when נ was pronounced as well as written; the next step was to assimilate it to the following consonant, but to retain it in writing, as was done in Syriac;[a] the final step was to eliminate the נ in writing, since it was no longer pronounced. This process did not take place in all the words of any one language simultaneously, and some words reached the final stage while in others the נ was still pronounced. The comparative infrequency of assimilation in BA shows this to be an early stage in the development of the language, yet one which was considerably advanced beyond the earliest form of Aramaic.

[a] See above, § 16.

23. Doubling results in BA, as in Hebrew, from the suppression of א or ה after a vowelless consonant. Hebrew forms like אוֹדֶנּוּ Ps. 42, 6, cf. יְבָרֲכֶנְהוּ Ps. 72, 15, are due to this process. The Hithpeʿel of verbs ע״ו is an example in BA; e. g., יִתְּזִין 4, 9 is to be explained as being really a Hit'aphʿal form, of which no example is extant in roots other than ע״ו (cf. Nöldeke, § 36; contrast Haupt, *SBOT.*, Ezra, p. 62). The Syriac form ܐܶܬܬܩܰܡܰܡ (ܐܬܩܡܡ), however, proves that we are dealing with a phonetic principle which existed in Aramaic independently of Hebrew. Talmudic איתמר, i. e., אִתְּמַר for אתאמר, is another illustration of the same principle; cf. Syriac ܐܶܬܬܡܰܪ (ܐܬܡܪ). In Arabic اِتَّخَذَ and similar forms (Wright, I, § 139) the doubling of the consonant compensates for the suppression of a preceding ا.

BA יְתִנִּנַּהּ 4, 14 is not analogous to יִתֶּנְנָּה Gen. 23, 9 for יִתְּנֶנָּה*, as proved by the position of the accent and by the mappiḳ in the הּ. In BA, as in Targumic and other Aramaic dialects (also occasionally in the inscriptions, cf. Lidzbarski, 404), the suffixes are joined in the imperfect to a form which corresponds to the Arabic second energetic (but with ָ in the place of َ). The suffix ־כוֹן, however, is joined, as ־כֶם occasionally in Hebrew, to the form corresponding to the first energetic.

24. BA shares with Hebrew the peculiarity of unorganic doubling of consonants for the purpose of protecting a Semitic short vowel in an open unaccented syllable.[a] An older period in both languages is to be distinguished in which the doubling served the additional purpose of increasing the volume of the form.[b] There is, however, no reason to suspect a Hebraism, as the phenomenon is met with also in Syriac.[c]

[a]The examples in BA are חֲנֻכַּת 3, 2, etc. (= Heb.); חַרְטֻמַּיָּא 2, 10, etc. (Heb. חַרְטֻמִּים); לִשָּׁנַיָּא 3, 4, etc. (cf. Syr. ܠܶܫܳܢܳܐ); פְלֻגָּתְהוֹן Ez. 6, 18 (cf. Heb. פְּלֻגּוֹת), אַרְכֻבָּתֵהּ 5, 6. The words חֲנֻכָּה and פְּלֻגָּה, however, may represent lexical Hebraisms, technical words from the temple liturgy and service; cf. also above, § 20, for another view.

[b]From this older period date the imperfect forms יִכֻּל 3, 29 and יִתִּב 7, 26; cf. in Hebrew regularly the forms of the imperfect of פ״י

verbs, the second radical of which is a sibilant; e. g., הִצִּית (rt. יצת); GK., § 93, 2, Rem. 1 and § 71). Elsewhere (the noun מַדָּע, which is perhaps an Aramaism [Kautzsch, *Aramaismen*, 51], excepted) in Hebrew, instead of the doubling of the second radical, the vowel of the prefix is modified in accordance with the usual rules applying to open unaccented syllables immediately preceding the accented syllable, and is treated as permanent even though the accent shifts; hence יֵדַע, יֵשֵׁב, יֵדָעֶנּוּ Jer. 17, 9.

Margolis (*AJSL.*, XIX [1903], 168) regards "יֵשֵׁב and יִתֵּב as parallel forms exactly as are דְּבָרִים and גְּמַלִּים; the permanency of the vowel of the prefix and the 'doubling' of the first radical serve, each in its way, to increase the volume of the biconsonantal basis of the imperfect stem." So also Brockelmann: "Das Streben, diese Formen den dreikonsonantigen anzugleichen, bewirkte in Syr. bei ܢܺܬܶܒ und ܢܺܕܰܥ Verdoppelung des 2 Radikals: ܢܶܬܶܒ, ܢܶܕܰܥ" (*Syr. Gram.*, § 192). In Syriac the doubling is found in these two verbs only, the other first ܝ verbs following the analogy of first ܘ verbs (Nöldeke, § 175). The principle thus belongs clearly to Aramaic in general (cf. also the Christian-Palestinian example referred to by Kautzsch, *Aramäismen*, 51; the rebuke which Kautzsch administers to Jacob in this work shows that he has here arrived at a clearer conception of the term "Hebraism" so freely used by him in his grammar of BA).

ᶜCf. in addition to ܟܽܣܶܐ referred to above, Syr. ܢܶܫ̈ܶܐ by the side of Targ. נְשַׁיָּא. Lagarde's view (*Übersicht*, 11) that the unorganic doubling in גְּמַלִּים, etc., is a mere device of the Masoretes for the purpose of squaring their system with the still living pronunciation, will hardly commend itself. He is also in the wrong in his explanation of Μεσσίας = מְשִׁיחָא* as a fi''il form with organic doubling (*Übersicht*, 93 ff.). The doubling, of course, is unorganic; note again that the consonant doubled is a sibilant; Μεσσίας by the side of מָשִׁיחַ is no more strange than ܟܽܣܶܐ by the side of לָשׁוֹן or ܢܶܫ̈ܶܐ by the side of נָשִׁים; Μεσσίας, therefore, merely represents the Aramaic—i. e., popular—form; Kautzsch, art. "Messiah," *EB.*, col. 3057, correctly compares the Greek transcription.

25. In BA as in Hebrew the plural of בַּיִת takes *dagesh* in the ת; e. g., בָּתֵּיכוֹן 2, 5; cf. בָּתִּים Ex. 1, 21; בָּתֵּיכֶם Gen. 42, 19, etc. Kautzsch at first regarded this as a pure Hebraism (*GBA.*, 12 *c*). His later opinion, however, is that, in view of the fact that Syriac also has ܬ after the vowel (Nöldeke, § 146;

Mand., § 148), the *dagesh* is due to the character of the form. This is the opinion also of Behrmann (commentary, p. 8).

Whatever may be the true explanation of the *dagesh*, the Syriac and Mandaic prove that the form in BA is not a Hebraism. Wright (*Comp. Gram.*, 88) regards the *dagesh* in the תּ as *d. lene*, and reads בָּתִּים bātīm; so also does Brockelmann (*Syr. Gram.*, § 123, Anm. 1); the analogy of the singular to which he refers, however, falls to the ground, since the explosive after a diphthong is peculiar to Syriac (late Aramaic) and is not shared by BA; cf. בַּיְתָא Ez. 5, 3. Nöldeke (*Merx's Archiv*, I, 456 ff.; *Mand.*, § 148), on the other hand, regards the point as *d. forte* and reads bāttīm. Cf. also König, *Lehrgeb.*, II, 56; Philippi, *ZDMG.*, XLIX (1895), 206.

26. Transposition of consonants takes place in BA as in Hebrew, in the reflexive (BA passive) stems when the ת of the preformative immediately precedes a sibilant.

The examples are: תִּשְׁתְּבִק 2, 44; מִשְׁתַּבְּשִׁין 5, 9; אֶשְׁתַּדּוּר Ez. 4, 15. 19; יִשְׁתַּוֵּה 3, 29; הִשְׁתְּכַה 6, 24; Ez. 6, 2; הִשְׁתְּכַחַת 2, 35; 5, 11. 12. 14. 27; 6, 5. 23; אֶשְׁתּוֹמַם 4, 16; יִשְׁתַּמְּעוּן 7, 27; אִשְׁתַּנִּו 3, 19; יִשְׁתַּנֵּא 2, 9; יִשְׁתַּנּוֹ 5, 10; יִשְׁתַּנּוֹן 7, 28; מִשְׁתָּרַיִן 5, 6; and in the Ishtaph'al יִשְׁתַּכְלְלוּן Ez. 4, 13. 16; מִשְׁתַּכַּל 7, 8. In the *kerē* הִזְדַּמִּנְתּוּן 2. 9, and in יִצְטַבַּע 5, 21, there is not only transposition, but the ת is changed to ד and ט respectively in "partial assimilation" to the first radical. (See for the Hebrew, GK., § 54, 2; cf. also Sievers, *Phonetik*[5], 1901, § 751.)

27. This, however, is in accordance with regular Semitic usage. Cf. the Syriac, ܐܙܕܕܩ, ܐܣܬܟܠ, etc. (Nöldeke, § 26; Brockelmann, § 89). Wright regards إِقْتَتَلَ, the Arabic VIII form as a development from this transposition, "which began with the verbs which commenced with a sibilant, and was gradually extended to all alike" (*Comp. Gr.*, 208).

28. In BA syncope of ה sometimes takes place in the Haph'el after the preformative of the imperfect and participle.

Following are the examples: מְגִידָךְ 7, 2; תַּדִּק 2, 40. 44; תַּהֶקְנֵּה 7, 23; מַדְּקָה 7, 7. 19; מַהְלְכִין 3, 25. 34 (the reading מְהַלְּכִין is preferred by Strack, Kamphausen, Marti); יְהִיטוּ Ez. 4, 12 (the form is somewhat doubtful; cf. Kautzsch, § 16, 5 Anm.; Fraenkel, *ZAW.*,

XIX (1889), 180; Batten, *SBOT.*, Ezra, p. 62); מַחֵא 5, 19; יַחְסְנוּן 7, 18; מַחְצְפָה 3, 22; תַּטְלֵל 4, 9; מוֹדֵא 6, 11; תַּחֵת Ez. 6, 5; מַצַּל 6, 28; תְּסֵק 2, 44; מַצְלַח Ez. 5, 8; מַצְלְחִין Ez. 6, 14; יְקִים 2, 44; 4, 14; תְּקִים 6, 9; מָרִים 5, 19; מַשְׁפִּל 5, 19; יְתִיבוּן 5, 5.

29. The ה is retained, however, in the following examples:

Haph'el, imperfect: 3d masc. sing., יְהַחֲוֵה 5, 12; יְהוֹדַע 2, 25; יְהוֹדְעִנַּנִי 7, 16; יְהָקֵים 5, 21; 6, 16; יְהַשְׁנֵא Ez. 6, 11; יְהַשְׁפִּל 7, 24; 3d fem. sing., תְּהַנְזִק Ez. 4, 13; 2d masc. sing., תְּהוֹבֵד 2, 24; תְּהַשְׁכַּח Ez. 4, 15; 7, 16; 1st sing. אֲהוֹדְעִנֵּהּ 5, 17; 3d. pl. masc., יְהוֹבְדוּן 2, 18; יְהוֹדְעוּן 2, 30; יְהוֹדְעֻנַּנִי 4, 3; יְהַעְדּוֹן 7, 26; יְהַתִיבוּן Ez. 6, 5; 2d masc. pl., תְּהַחֲוֹן 2, 6; תְּהַחֲוֻנַּנִי 2, 9; תְּהוֹדְעוּן Ez. 7, 25; תְּהוֹדְעֻנַּנִי 2, 5. 9; 1st pl. נְהַחֲוֵה 2, 7; נְהַשְׁכַּח 6, 6. Haph'el participle: masc. מְהֵימַן 2, 45; 6, 5; מְהַדֵּק 2, 40; מְהוֹדֵא 2, 23; מְהַעְדֵּה 2, 21; מְהָקֵים 2, 21; מְהַשְׁנֵא 2, 21; fem. מְהַחְצְפָה 2, 15: מְהַנְזְקַת Ez. 4, 15; pl. מְהוֹדְעִין 4, 4; Ez. 4, 16; 7, 24: מְהַחֲתִין Ez. 6, 1; מְהַקְרְבִין Ez. 6, 10.

30. In the Aramaic inscriptions ה is usually syncopated in the imperfect and participles of the Haph'el,[a] although in a few places it is retained.[b]

[a] With syncope of ה, יאגר Na., 220, 4; 224, 9; יוגר Na., 197, 6; 199, 6; 206, 4; 214, 5; 217, 6; יוגרון Na., 212, 3; מחרם Na., 206, 3; מודא Pa., Vog. 79, 2; 80, 2; and frequently fem. מודיא Pa., Vog. 83 *a*, 2; *b*, 2; pl. מודן Pa., Vog. 93, 1; impf. with suff. יכילנה Pa., T., II, *b*, 23; ינפק Na., 197, 2; 198, 5. 9; 206, 5; 207, 3; part. act. מפק Pa., T., II, *a*, 31; *b*, 31 ff.; part. act. pl. מפקא *ibid.*, II, *b*, 47; part. act. מפל *ibid.*, II, *b*, 30; part. pl. st. c. מפלי *ibid.*, II, *a*, 1; part. act. fem. s. מקבלא Pa., Nöldeke, 6; יקם Had., 28; ישאל Na. 206, 4.

[b] With ה or א retained: יהאברו Nerāb 1, 11; יהבאשו Nerāb 2, 9; part. pass. מאפק Pa., T., II, *c*, 12; [פק] יהנ 113, 21.

31. In Hebrew the ה is regularly syncopated in the imperfect and participle. Occasionally, however, the ה is retained in the imperfect, as יְהוֹשִׁיעַ for יוֹשִׁיעַ, I Sam. 17, 47 (GK., § 53 *q*). In Syriac, likewise, the ܐ of the prefix disappears after prefixes in the imperfect, participle, and infinitive (Nöldeke, § 164). Similarly, ܗ disappears in forms of the verb ܗܠܟ (Nöldeke, § 183). In Arabic, when أ is used as the preformative of the IV perfect, it is syncopated in the imperfect

and participle, but, when ܫ is used, it is retained and the verb is treated as a quadriliteral. Thus هَرَاقَ impf. يُهَرِيقُ, etc. (cf. Wright, I, § 118, Rem. b; *Comp. Gram.*, 205; Zimmern, 20; also above, § 11).

32. In BA א is syncopated when preceded by a reduced vowel or by a closed syllable.[a] The same phenomenon occurs in Hebrew,[b] and is very frequent in Syriac.[c] Caution is necessary, since forms with quiescent א may be the original ones, while those with the א sounded and a preceding ֲ may be resolutions.[d]

[a] E. g., בֵּאישְׁתָּא Ez. 4, 12 (for בִּאְישְׁתָּא); גֵּוָה 4, 34 (for גְּאֵוָה); מָרֵאי 4, 16 (for מְרָאִי); מַלַּאת 2, 35 (for מְלָאַת).

[b] E. g., מָאתַיִם Gen. 11, 23 (for מְאָתַיִם*); אֲחַטֶּנָּה Gen. 31, 39 (for אֲחַטְּאֶנָּה), etc. (Stade, § 111.)

[c] ܡܳܐܠܳܐ for ܡܐܠܐ; ܬܡܳܢܝܐ for ܬܡܐܢܝܐ; with the ܐ omitted in writing: ܨܳܡ, ܡܰܠܶܦ cf. Heb. מַלְּפֵנוּ Job 35, 11 (Nöldeke, § 33). Note, however, the practice of the Eastern Syrians (*ibid.*).

[d] E. g., שֵׁאת in לְשֵׂאת is certainly more original than שְׂאֵת. On רְאֵם, etc., cf. below, § 58.

33. As in Hebrew, so in BA the laryngeals (א, ה, ח, ע) and ר may cause modifications in the vowels preceding or following them. Thus, since they cannot be doubled, in certain cases a preceding vowel comes to stand in an open syllable and may be modified;[a] sometimes, however, it is not so modified.[b]

[a] Cf. below, § 46, 15.

[b] So-called virtual doubling, the frequency of which decreases, while the frequency of vowel modification increases, in the order ח, ה, ע, א, ר. Thus we have virtual doubling with ח always; with ה in eight out of nine cases (contrast מִתְבְּהָל 5, 9 with יְבַהֲלֻךְ 4, 16, etc.); with ע in seven out of nine cases; with ר in only one (אֲרִיךְ Ez. 4, 14) out of twenty-two cases. No examples with א are available.

For the Hebrew see GK., § 22 *c*. The tendency in Hebrew is for ע to reject the doubling altogether. On ר cf. GK., § 22 *q*, and particularly *s*; add הֶרָה Gen. 14, 10 (for הַרָה*). In Syriac it is questionable how far ܚ and ܗ undergo a true doubling. The vocalization, however, is as though such took place (e. g., ܫܰܪܳܪ). The Eastern Syrians very early ceased to double ܪ, and in consequence frequently modified a preceding *a* to *ā* (Nöldeke, § 21 A).

34. As in Hebrew, *i* and *u* preceding a laryngeal or ר are often changed to *a*. While in Hebrew, however, the phonetic change is confined to closed syllables, BA goes a step further in permitting it also in open accented syllables.

The examples are found in the perf. of فَعِلَ verbs (e. g., תְּוַהּ 3, 24, שְׁמַע 6, 15 [Arabic سَمِعَ], שְׁפַר 3, 32); in the part.-act. Pe'al (e. g., יָדַע 2, 8; cf. Heb. נֹטַע אֹזֶן Ps. 94, 9; the corresponding Hebrew form here as in all nouns is to be looked for in the cstr. state with which the cstr. and absol. states in BA coincide, while in the absol. state Hebrew goes its own way in producing pausal forms which BA does not recognize); and in the (perf., imperf., imper., and—differing from the Hebrew—participle active of the) Pa'ēl, Haph'ēl (for the corresponding Hebrew forms use the jussive), and Hithpe'el (e. g., בַּהֲלוּנַּהּ 4, 11; יְבַקַּר Ez. 4, 15; שַׁבַּחוּ 5, 4; מְפַשַּׁר 5, 12; הַצְלַח 3, 30; יְהוֹדַע 2, 23; אַתַּרוּ 4, 11; מַצְלַח Ez. 5, 8; הִשְׁתְּכַח 2, 35). The Hithpa'al forms are purposely ignored, as Hithpa'el forms are an anomaly peculiar to Hebrew only (cf. Arabic تَقَتَّلَ, يَتَقَتَّلُ, and Hebrew pausal forms, GK, § 54). In the prefix of the impf. Pe'al (e. g., תַּעַבְדוּן Ez. 6, 8, cf. Heb. יַעַבְדוּ Dt. 12, 30) the original vowel is apparently preserved (cf. Arabic يَقْتُلُ). Equally to be ignored is the *a* in the imperf. Pe'al of فَعَلَ verbs with a laryngeal as third radical (cf. תְּהַנְדַּע 2, 30 [Heb. תֵּדַע]; יִשְׁלַח Ez. 5, 17 [Heb. יִשְׁלַח]), which as a possibility comes from common Semitic times (cf. Syr. ܢܶܦܬܰܚ, Arabic يَسْأَلُ, يَفْتَحُ, etc.; cf. Vernier, I, § 146, 20; Wright, I, § 91, Rem. a). In יִשְׁמַע 3. 10 the ַ is, of course, original and not the result of the influence of the laryngeal ע; cf. Arabic يَسْمَعُ (cf. Wright, I, § 92).

35. The same phonetic changes occur in Syriac; cf. perf. of the type فَعِلَ, ܫܡܰܥ, etc.; part. ܫܳܡܰܥ, Pa'el ܦܰܪܶܣ, ܢܦܰܪܶܣ, ܦܰܪܶܣ, ܡܦܰܪܶܣ, corresponding to ܫܰܡܶܗ, ܢܫܰܡܶܗ, ܫܰܡܶܗ, ܡܫܰܡܶܗ, etc.; 'Aph'ēl ܐܰܫܡܰܥ, ܢܰܫܡܰܥ, etc., corresponding to ܐܰܫܡܶܗ, etc.;

Ethpe'el ܐܶܬܦܪܶܥ. There are no traces of the vowel *a* in the prefix of the impf. Pe'al in Syriac (Brockelmann, § 182[1]). With regard to the imperf of فَعَلَ verbs with a laryngeal as third radical, Syriac agrees with Arabic, rather than with Hebrew and BA, in allowing the vowel *u* to remain quite frequently (Brockelmann, § 186).

36. In BA as in Hebrew א is subject to quiescence when closing a syllable. This occurs in (1) nouns of the type of roots فَعْل;[a] (2) nouns with a formative prefix, e. g., מ (hence in BA infinitives) and verbal forms with a prefix (impf. Ḳal [Pe'al]; in Hebrew also the Niph'al and Hiph'il) of פ״א roots;[b] (3) nouns or verbs of פ״א roots with proclitic prefixes.[c]

[a]E. g., רֵאשׁ (Heb. רֹאשׁ) 7, 1; מָאנַיָּא Ez. 5, 15. מָאן* is probably only a secondary فَعْل form = مَأْن = مَأْنَى; cf. Lagarde, *Übersicht*, 184. We eliminate proper names like בֵּלְשַׁאצַּר 5, 1, etc., which are borrowed from Assyrian.

[b]E. g., מֵאמַר 4, 14; מֹאזַנַיָּא 5, 27 (Heb. מֹאזְנַיִם Is. 40, 15); לְמֵאמַר 2, 9, hence also with the א lost in writing לְמֵמַר Ez. 5, 11; cf. also לְמֵזֵא 3, 19 and לְמֵתֵא 3, 2; יֵאבַדוּ Jer. 10, 11 (Heb. יֹאבְדוּ Jud. 5, 31); יֵאכֻל 4, 30 (Heb. יֹאכַל Gen. 49, 27); יֵאמַר 2, 7 (Heb. יֹאמַר Gen. 31, 8). For Hebrew examples in the Niph'al and Hiph'il cf. GK., § 68 *i*. BA תְּהוֹבֵד 2, 14, however, as may be seen from Syriac, ܢܶܘܒܶܕ, etc., is to be explained as an analogical formation induced by the פ״ו class.

[c]E. g., בֵּאדַיִן 2, 14; בֵּאלָהֵהּ 6, 24; לֵאלָהָא 5, 23; וֵאלָהָא Ez. 6, 12 (for Hebrew examples cf. GK., §§ 102 *d*, 104 *d*). On the other hand, cf. בַּאֲסוּר 4. 12; כַּאֲנָשׁ 7, 4; לַאֲלָהּ 2, 19; וַאֲדַיִן Ez. 5, 7 for בְּאֱסוּר*, כְּאֱנָשׁ*, לְאֱלָהּ* and וְאֱדַיִן*. It is incorrect to derive forms like יֵאמַר and the like (as does Kautzsch, § 11, 3 *b*) from יֶאֱמַר, etc. The truth is that we are dealing with two sets of forms, those with quiescent א and those with א retaining its consonantal force. When once the א quiesced, the syllable which it closed became opened, and its vowel was treated accordingly (cf. below, § 46). Where א retained its consonantal force, it is self-evident that forms like וְאֱדַיִן preceded those like וַאֲדַיִן. To say that יֵאמַר comes from יֶאֱמַר is to say that the א retains its consonantal force and at the same time quiesces.

37. In the Aramaic inscriptions it is difficult to tell whether the א which is written is also meant to be sounded. Since, however, we find (just in one example) the א omitted (after the prefix א), the inference is legitimate that elsewhere the א is meant to be pronounced.

The examples are: תאבד Ner. 2, 10; יאחז Hadad 15. 20. 25; אחז (first per. sing.) *ibid.* 3; יאכל 145 A, 4; תאכל Hadad 21; יאכלו 137 B, 3; inf. לאכל Hadad 23; תאלב *ibid.*, 34; יאמר *ibid.*, 17. 21. 29 (twice); יאמרון 45 D, 8; יאתא Na., 217, 2 (219, 4).

38. In Syriac we unquestionably meet with the same phenomenon as in BA.

Examples: ܥܢܐ (Heb. צאן, Arabic ضَأْن); ܒܐܪܐ = *bi'r-ā (on Heb. בְּאֵר, etc., cf. below, § 58); ܪܫܐ (observe the phonetic spelling; next step ܪܫܐ); ܬܐܠܦ; ܬܐܡܪ, ܬܐܟܘܠ; ܬܐܡܪܘܢ; ܬܐܡܪ (Brockelmann, §§ 68. 191 *b*); ܢܐܡܪ (Nöldeke, § 33, who unnecessarily confounds it with ܐܡܪ and similar cases).

39. In Arabic likewise the *hamzah* is subject to quiescence; e. g., رَاسٌ for رَأْسٌ, بِيرٌ for بِئْرٌ. Quiescence necessarily takes place after the prefix أ, as أَأْمَنَ or آمَنَ (i. e., the quiescent ا is lost also in writing), etc. The Arab grammarians refer to the loss of the consonantal force of ا as "lightening of the *hamzah*" (تَخْفِيفُ ٱلْهَمْزَةِ: Wright, I, 18 D; cf. *Mufaṣṣal*, 198 ff.). In the dialect of Hijaz in the time of Mohammed the *taḫfīf* was quite general even when other consonants than ا preceded the *hamzah* (cf. footnote in Wright, I, 72 D; also Nöldeke, *Geschichte des Qorans*, 1860, 345 ff.).

40. It is thus clear that the loss of the consonantal force of א began in the common Semitic period. Excepting in the dialect of Hijaz, it is rather rare in Arabic; Hebrew comes next with its examples of the quiescent א; then BA; and last of all Syriac, in which, when reference is had to the examples of syncope (cf. above, § 32), the loss of ܐ in sound is the rule. With Syriac go the modern dialects of Arabic (Spitta, § 5; Vollers-Burkitt, §§ 91 ff.).

41. ו and י, when closing a syllable, represent in BA as well as in Hebrew consonantal u̯ and i̯ (corresponding to the sonants *u* and *i*; for the term "consonantal" and "sonant" cf. Brugmann, I, 35; Philippi, "Die Aussprache der semit. Konsonanten ו und י," *ZDMG.*, XL [1886], 639 ff.; Haupt, "Über die beiden Halbvocale u̯ and i̯," *BSS.*, I [1889], 255–293 ff.; Philippi, "Nochmals die Aussprache d. semit. Consonanten ו und י," *ZDMG.*, LI [1897], 66 ff.), and coalesce with a homogeneous vowel into the corresponding sonants *ū* and *ī*,[a] while with a heterogeneous vowel they form a diphthong. The diphthong thus formed may remain uncontracted or be contracted into a monophthong.[b]

[a] Eg., יוּכַל 2, 20 (Heb. יוּכַל Gen. 31, 16; cf. below, § 65); הוּסְפַת 4, 33 (cf. Heb. הוּרַד Gen. 39, 1), etc. No examples for *ī* (cf. Heb. יִירַשׁ Gen. 21, 10, etc.) are found in BA, וִיקָר 2, 6; לִיקַר 4, 33; וִיהַבוּ 3, 38; בִּידַיִן 2, 34, etc., originating in וְ+יְקָר, etc., i. e., initial יְ was pronounced *ī*.

[b] We meet with a diphthong always after a (Semitic) long vowel, e. g., שַׁפִּיר 3, 28 (cf. Heb. זִו I Kings 6, 1), or a long vowel which is the resultant of a Semitic diphthong, e. g., חֵיוְתָא 7, 6; and after ֵ originating in Semitic *i*, e. g., לְשְׁלֵוְתָךְ 4, 24 (cf. Heb. שָׁלֵו Job 16, 12); also after a parasitic ֶ e. g., לֶהֱוֵין 5, 17. The vowel *a* combines into a diphthong with ו as well as with י. In Hebrew *au̯* and *ai̯* may and may not be contracted when followed by no vowelless consonant, hence עַוְלָתָה Job 26, 30 by the side of עֹלָתָה Job 5, 16; מַיְמִינִים I Chron. 12, 2 by the side of הֵימִינִי Ezek. 21, 21. The contraction, however, is uniformly avoided in Hebrew (as in BA and Syriac, and also in modern Arabic) when the u̯ or i̯ is doubled, e. g., חַיָּה Gen. 2, 7 (hence also in חַיְיַהְוָה for חַיְיַהְוֶה; Sievers, I, 296, footnote), etc. While חַי is the correct form for the absolute state, וָחַי Gen. 3, 22 is a (semi-) pausal and וְחֵי Lev. 25, 36 is a construct state (not in the sense of GK., § 76 *i*, but in that given to the term by Margolis, *AJSL.*, XIX [1902], 169). יָדַי II Sam. 22, 21 = يَدَيَّ (Wright, I, § 317) is prevented from becoming יָדֵי* by the impetus of the original doubling, or, as it may be said in the usual parlance of our grammars, the י is *virtually doubled;* contrast יְדֵי Gen. 24, 30 = يَدَيْ. Cf. BA גַּוַּהּ 4, 15, contrast גּוֹא (with otiose א) cstr. state 3, 25; ܓܰܘܳܐ Nöldeke, § 102; cf. Spitta, § 17 *b*). When fol-

lowed by a vowelless consonant, hence when in a doubly closed syllable (GK., § 26 *d*), contraction is the rule if the loss of the (Semitic) vowel following the closing consonant occurs in the middle of a word (the construct state properly not counting as a separate word), as in צֹמְכֶם Is. 58, 3, בֵּיתְכֶם Num. 18, 31, מוֹת (cstr. state) Gen. 25, 11, בֵּית (cstr. state) *ibid.*, 12, 15. If, on the other hand, the loss of the vowel occurs in pause (Vernier, I, § 126)—hence in the absolute state (cf. Margolis, *AJSL.*, XII [1896], 203)—the proper Hebrew method requires an uncontracted diphthong, which is made possible by the insertion of a parasitic vowel; hence מָוֶת Deut. 19, 6, בַּיִת Ez. 12, 30, רַגְלַיִם Is. 28, 3 = *maut, bait, raglaim,* = *maut-a* (accus.), *bait-a* (accus.), *ragl-ai-mi* (or *-ma*, cf. the dialectal form *-ai-na*, Wright, I, 235 n.). Contracted forms in the absolute state, e. g., צוֹם II Sam. 12, 6, do not violate the principle just stated, as in such cases the construct state has been made to do service for the absolute (as is the case in Aramaic always—an "Aramaism" in Hebrew). In BA no example is available of uncontracted *au*. When not followed by a vowelless consonant the diphthong *ai* appears uncontracted more frequently in BA than in Hebrew, e. g., בַּיְתֵהּ 3, 29; חֲזַיְתָ 2, 41, הַיְתִי 5, 13, etc.; but cf. בְּעֵינָא 2, 23: דָמֵינָא 3, 24, בֵּינֵיהוֹן 7, 8, הֵיכַל Ez. 5, 14, etc. When followed by a vowelless consonant not in pause, contraction is the rule as in Hebrew, e. g., לֵילְיָא 5, 30; סוֹף (cstr. state) 4, 8; בֵּית (cstr. state) 4, 27, הֱוֵית 4, 1, etc. In pause, we find on the one hand, as in Hebrew, חַיִל 3, 20 קַיִט 2, 35; רַגְלַיִן 7, 4, קַרְנַיִן 7, 7 (cf., however, בָּנַיִן Ez. 4, 12 [plural of the participle = **bānai-īn*]; Kautzsch, § 47 *g*, *e* rightly compares the Heb. plurals מַיִם and שָׁמַיִם, to which add the traditional מַעַיִם, in the texts מעיים); on the other, יוֹם (absol. st.) Ez. 6, 9, that is, the constr. state replaces the proper absolute state form. Philippi, *ZDMG.*, LI (1897), 83, n. 3, neglects to account for חַיִל, קַרְנַיִן, etc. The ָ in the examples just referred to is correctly explained by Brockelmann, *ZDMG.*, 58 (1904), 523, against Foote, *J. H. U. Circulars*, No. 163, June, 1903, 70 ff., who looks upon the point as an equivalent to שְׁוָא. The forms of the *Kethibh* לעבדיך (k לְעַבְדָיִךְ) 2, 4, etc., are to be read accordingly לְעַבְדַיִךְ, etc. The contraction is analogous to Heb. דֹּתָן Gen. 37, 17 by the side of דֹּתַיְנָה *ibid.* The loss of the final vowel in לעבדיך occurred, however, in late Aramaic.

42. In Syriac we meet with the same phenomenon.

E. g., ܡܘܬܐ for ܡܘܘܬܐ, ܡܝܬ, written also ܐܡܝܬ, hence ܡܝܬܬ (ܐܡܝܬܬ), etc.; also in the middle of a word ܬܡܝܬܘܢ, ܡܝܬܘܗܝ. With regard to *au̯* and *ai̯*, Syriac presents the contraction in doubly closed syllables, no account being taken of pause (i. e., the cstr. state (sing.) is used also for the absolute), e. g., ܬܘܪܬܐ, ܡܘܬ, ܝܘܡܬ, ܒܝܬ, ܬܝܡܢ, ܥܠܝܟܝܢ, etc. In the middle of a word, when followed by no vowelless consonant, the diphthong remains uncontracted, e. g., ܒܝܬܐ, ܝܘܡܐ, etc., although here likewise the contraction occurs in Eastern Syriac and in Mandaic, not, however, to the exclusion of the uncontracted diphthongs (cf. Nöldeke, § 49 A; *Mand.*, 21 f., 258, 246 f.; note the fluctuating orthography עותבאן and אותבאן and cf. for the principle of orthography, p. 7). ܝܘܡܬܢ is correctly interpreted by Nöldeke (§ 49 A) as a late form in Syriac; ܥܠܝܟܘܢ, ܥܠܝܟܝܢ, ܥܒܕܝܟܝܢ likewise were probably late; ܥܒܕܝܟܝ, however, is on a line with BA לעבדיך k. In ܝܘܡܬܗܘܢ, however, Syriac goes its own way. The form is due probably to analogy with ܝܘܡܬܟܘܢ, etc. (so correctly Philippi, *loc. cit.*).

43. In modern Arabic the contraction of the diphthongs *au̯* and *ai̯* into *ō* and *ē* is the rule in some regions, e. g., *i̯ōm* يَوْمٌ, *'ēn* عَيْنٌ, *īdēn* يَدَيْنِ, etc., although examples occur with the diphthongs kept uncontracted (Spitta, § 17).

44. Semitic *ā* appears in BA as ָ, whereas in Hebrew it is represented by וֹ, as, e. g., אָמַר 2, 5 (Heb. אֹמֵר Gen. 32, 10, Arab. آمِرٌ). In a few instances, however, we meet in BA with the Hebrew וֹ. The examples are:

אנושא (k) 4, 13. 14 (אֲנָשָׁא k), cf. Heb. אֱנוֹשׁ Is. 8, 1; הַרְהֹרִין 4, 2 (contrast Syriac ܗܪܗܪܐ *mirage* PS, col. 1047; Baer, עבודת ישראל 1868, 573, incorrectly introduces the Aramaic הַרְהֹרִים for Heb. הרהורים); מְדֹרָךְ 4, 22, 29, מְדוֹרֵהּ 5, 21 (contrast מְדָרְהוֹן 2, 11); דִּכְרוֹנָה Ez. 6, 2, cf. Heb. זִכָּרוֹן Josh. 4, 7, and contrast דָּכְרָנַיָּא Ez. 4, 15; מָזוֹן 4, 9. 18, cf. Heb. מָזוֹן Gen. 45, 23; II Chron. 11, 23 (Dillmann, II, 409 regards מָזוֹן in Genesis as a gloss and the word as an Aramaic loan-word; it is frequent in Mishnaic Hebrew; cf. also below, § 45, n. 12); עֶלְיוֹנִין 7, 18, etc., cf. Heb. עֶלְיוֹן Gen. 14, 18; רַעְיוֹנֵי 2, 30; רַעְיוֹנַי 7, 28; רַעְיוֹנָךְ 2, 29; 5, 10; רַעְיֹנֹהִי 4, 16; 5, 6; cf. Heb. רַעְיוֹן Ecc. 1, 17 (an Aramaic loan-word; Kautzsch, *Aramaismen*, 82 f., contrasts ܪܥܝܢܐ); שִׁלְטֹנֵי 3, 2, etc., cf. Heb. שִׁלְטוֹן Ecc. 8, 4 (Aramaic loan-word, Kautzsch, *loc. cit.*, 88 ff.; contrast שָׁלְטָנַיָּא 7, 27); מֹאזַנְיָא 5, 27 cf. Heb. מֹאזְנַיִם Is. 40, 15 (from original *ma'zin* cf. above, § 36, a). Doubtful cases have been omitted.

45. There is no reason, however, to speak of this as a Hebraism. According to Lagarde (*Mittheil.*, I, § 80; *Übersicht*, 84, footnote **, 199, 200), Syriac ܨܗܝܘܢ (Heb. צִיּוֹן); ܓܠܝܘܢ (Heb. גִּלָּיוֹן Is. 8, 1); ܚܙܘܢ (Heb. חִזָּיוֹן II Sam. 7, 17); ܢܣܝܘܢ (cf. נסיון Sir. 13, 11 c) are loan-words from the Hebrew, recognized by the Hebrew $\bar{o}$. If so, Hebrew מָזוֹן, רַעְיוֹן and שִׁלְטוֹן, which are said to be Aramaic loan-words, were Hebraized in pronunciation after the Aramaic word had been introduced into the Hebrew. The fact, however, that we meet with דכרון Na., 163 A; 169, 1; 338; שלטונהם Na., 196, 5, and other examples in Christian Palestinian (*ZDMG.*, XXII [1868], 474), Samaritan (Barth, § 194 *c*), Syriac, and Mandaic in words which are not loan-words (Nöldeke, *Mand.*, § 21) indicates that in a definite area shared both by Hebrew and certain Aramaic dialects Semitic $\bar{a}$ was sounded as $\bar{o}$ (so Barth, *loc. cit.*).

46. The following table illustrates the treatment of Semitic short vowels in BA and Hebrew. Each language, however, seems to go its own way in several cases; and there is no occasion to speak of Hebrew influence where they agree.*

Arabic Vowel	Closed			Open			
	Unaccented		Accented	Unaccented			Accented or Opened
	Through Doubling[1]	By Simple Consonant		Near the Tone	Distant: After א, ה, ח, ע	Distant: After Other Consonants	
u/o ◌ُ	◌ֻ *u*[2] (◌ָ *o*)	◌ָ *o*[3] (◌ֻ *u*)	◌ֹ *ō*[4]	◌ֹ *ō*[12]	◌ֳ *ŏ*[13]	◌ְ[14]	◌ֹ *ō* (◌ֻ *u* / ◌ָ *o*)[15]
i/e ◌ِ	◌ִ *i*[5] (◌ֶ *e*)	◌ֶ *e* (◌ִ *i*)[6] (◌ַ *a*)[7]	◌ֵ *ē* (◌ֶ *é*)[8] (◌ַ *a*)[7]	◌ֵ *ē*[12]	◌ֱ *ĕ*[13] ◌ֲ *ă*	◌ְ[14]	◌ֵ *ē* (◌ִ *i*)[15] (◌ֶ *e*)
a ◌َ	◌ַ *a*[9]	◌ַ *a*[10]	◌ָ *å*[11] ◌ַ *a*	◌ָ *å*[12] ◌ַ *a*	◌ֲ *ă*[13]	◌ְ[14]	◌ָ *å* (◌ַ *a*)[15] (◌ֶ *æ*)

*The table, enlarged so as to include Aramaic, follows the table prepared for Hebrew by Margolis and printed *AJSL.*, XIX (1903), 164; consult the footnotes (on the

[1] The doubling may be organic, or artificial to preserve an exceptional vowel.

[2] E. g., גַּבָּא 6, 17; אֻשַּׁיָּא Ez. 4, 12; אֻמָּה 3, 29; אֻמַּיָּא 3, 4; חֲנֻכַּת 3, 31; הֻסַּק 6, 24. Cf., however, כָּלְּהוֹן 2, 38 and כָּלְּהֵון 7, 19. Cf. Hebrew חֻקִּים Deut. 4, 5; תְּסֻבֶּינָה Gen. 37, 7; נֻתַּץ Jud. 6, 28; הֻגַּד Ruth 2, 11; אֲחֻזָּה Lev. 13, 34. On the other hand, יְבֻזּוּם Zeph. 2, 9; חָגָּא Is. 19, 17; עָזִּי Ex. 15, 2; עֻזְּךָ Ps. 21, 2; (by the side of עֻזְּךָ Ps. 66, 3); יְחָנֵּנוּ Ps. 67, 2 (by the side of יְחֻנֶּנּוּ Is. 27, 11); מָרַּת Prov. 14, 10; שָׁדְּדָה Na. 3, 7 (by the side of שֻׁדְּדָה Jer. 4, 20); כָּלּוּ Ps. 72, 20 (cf. וַיְכֻלּוּ Gen. 2, 1); כָּרַּת Ezek. 16, 4. Cf. in Syriac such examples as ܢܶܦܩܽܘܢ, ܪܽܘܚܳܐ, ܟܽܘܠܳܐ (Nöldeke, § 104), ܦܽܘܩܕܳܢܳܐ (§ 121), ܩܽܘܕܫܳܐ (§ 104).

[3] E. g., הָנְחַת 5, 20; הָתְקְנַת 4, 33; נָגְהָא 6, 20; שָׁרְשׁוֹהִי 4, 12; תָּקְפָּא 2, 37; אָרְחָתָךְ 5, 23; חָכְמְתָה 5, 11; חָכְמַת 5, 11; חָכְמְתָא 2, 20; כָּל־ 2, 10. Cf., however, כֻּתְלַיָּא Ez. 5, 8; גֻּבְרִין 3, 8; גֻּבְרַיָּא 3, 12 (in the last two cases the ֻ is due to the following labial). Cf. Hebrew אָזְנִי I Sam. 20, 2; מָלְכִי Jud. 9, 10; הָפְקַד Lev. 5, 23: תָּקְטָר Lev. 6, 15; חָק־ Lev. 6, 15; וַיָּקָם Gen. 4, 8. On the other hand קֻמְצוֹ Lev. 2, 2; קֻצְרְכֶם Lev. 19, 9; מֻשְׁלָךְ II Sam. 20, 21; אֻמְנָם Gen. 18, 13 (by the side of אָמְנָם Ruth 3, 12). Cf. such Syriac forms as ܩܽܘܪܒܳܐ, ܫܽܘܪܒܳܐ, ܢܽܘܩܒܳܐ, ܐܽܘܪܚܳܐ, etc. (Nöldeke, § 103); ܟܽܠ (§ 104) but also ܟܽܠ = kol (§ 48).

[4] E. g., גֹּב 6, 8; כֹּל 6, 8; דֹּב 7, 5; קֹשֹׁט 4, 34; חַרְטֹם 2, 10; כֹּלָּא 2, 40 shows that it matters not whether the syllable be closed with a simple or double consonant. Cf. Hebrew כֹּל Gen. 2, 5; קָטֹנְתִּי Gen. 32, 11; יִקְצֹף Lev. 10, 6; יָבֹזּוּ Is. 10, 2. Cf. Syriac ܟܽܠ (§ 104); ܢܶܩܛܽܘܠ, ܢܶܦܽܘܩ (§ 103); ܬܶܣܓܽܘܕ, ܢܶܣܓܽܘܕ (§ 160). Cf., however, יִסְגֻּד 3, 6; תִּרְשֻׁם 6, 9; פְּרֻק 4, 24; יֵאכֻל 4, 30; תֵּאכֻל 7, 23; יְכֻל 3, 29 and contrast Syriac ܢܶܣܓܽܘܠ (Nöldeke, § 48, is uncertain as to the value of the ܘ; cf. also Brockelmann, § 46).

[5] E. g., מִלְּתָה 2, 25; עִדָּנָא 2, 9; יִפֵּל 3, 6; יִתְנְכֵּה 4, 14; הִמּוֹן 2, 34; הִמּוֹ Ez. 5, 11; אִנּוּן Ez. 5, 4; יְהַחִנְפֵּה 2, 11; יִתְּזִין 4, 9; יִתְּשָׂמוּן 2, 5; לְשִׁנַּיָּא 3, 7. Cf., however, אֻשָּׁא 7, 11. Cf. Hebrew אִמְּי Gen.

page referred to) for an explanation of the terms used. The forms in parentheses occur less frequently.

20, 12; יִתֵּן Gen. 43, 14; אֶבְרָתוֹ Ps. 91, 4; מְבַעֲתֶךָ I Sam. 16, 15; חֲמִשָּׁה Gen. 18, 28; גִּדֵּל Jos. 4, 14. But cf. אֶקַּח Gen. 12, 19; אֶשָּׁעֵן Jud. 16, 26; אֶנָּחֵם Is. 1, 24 but אִנָּקְמָה Is. 1, 24; אִמָּלְטָה Gen. 19, 20; אִדָּרֵשׁ Ezek. 14, 3, etc. In Syriac ܵ is invariably used before doubling.

[6] There is in BA, as little as in Hebrew, a fixed rule as to when to use ַ and when ִ to represent an Arabic َ in an unaccented closed syllable. Thus in BA תִּמְהַיָּא 3, 22 (فَعْل, cf. Heb. תִּמָּה, i. e., תִּמָּה Si. 16, 11, the form inferred from תִּמָּהוֹן Zech. 12, 4, cf. *AJSL.*, XII (1896), 215) בִּשְׂרָא 2, 11 (فَعَل, cf. Heb. בָּשָׂר Gen. 2, 24); כִּדְנָה 2, 10 (=*ka-din-ā); יִקִּדְתָּא 3, 6; מִשְׁכְּבִי 4, 2; מִבְעֵא 2, 18; נִדְבָּכִין Ez. 6, 4; סִלְקַת 7, 20; שִׁמְעַת 5, 14; יִסְגֻּד 3, 6; תִּשְׁלַט 2, 39; יִנְתֵּן־ 2, 16; יְשֵׁיזְבִנְכוֹן 3, 15; הִזְדְּמִנְתּוּן 2, 9; but יַבֶּשְׁתָּא 2, 10 (=יַבִּישְׁתָּא=יַבֶּשְׁתָּא, cf. Syriac ܝܰܒܺܝܫܬܳܐ; ܝܰܒܺܝܫ is a by-form of يَابِس [from which يَابِسَة], of which יַבֵּשׁ* [from which יַבָּשָׁה Gen. 1, 9] is an intensive [nominal] form; just as גַּנָּב Ex. 22, 1 is the intensive of גֹּנֵב Ex. 21, 16; another by-form of ܝܰܒܺܝܫ is יָבֵשׁ Na. 1, 10); נִבְרַשְׁתָּא 5, 5; יִדְּהֹם Ez. 5, 8; נִפְקַת 2, 13; יִשְׁאֲלֻנְכוֹן Ez. 7, 21; מִתְעֲבֵד־ Ez. 4, 19; יִפֵּל־ Ez. 7, 20. ַ, however, seems to be the rule, and ִ the exception.

Before and after the gutturals, א, ה, ח, and ע, ִ is more common, but there are examples with ַ, the fluctuation being greatest in the case of א: אֶדְרָע 4, 23; אֶצְבְּעָתָא 2, 21; אֶשְׁתַּדּוּר Ez. 4, 15; אַבְעָא 7, 16; אֶקְרֵא 5, 17; אֶשְׁתּוֹמַם 4, 16; but אִנְבֵּהּ 4, 18; אִנְדַּע 2, 9; אִתְיָעַטוּ 6, 8; אִתְכְּרִיַּת 7, 15; אִתְעֲקַרָה 7, 8; אִשְׁתַּנִּי 3, 19;— הִתְקְטְלָה 2, 13; הִתְמְלִי 3, 19; הִשְׁתְּכַח 2, 35;—חֶדְוָא Ez. 6, 16; הֶזְוָא 2, 19; חֶלְמָא 2, 4; but חַסְנָא 2, 37; חַנְטִין Ez. 6, 9;—עֶלְיוֹנִין 7, 18; מֶעְבַּד Ez. 4, 22; יֶעְדֵּה 7, 14; הֶעְדִּיו 5, 20; but עַשְׂבָּא 4, 30; עִלְּעִין 7, 5. The same obtains in Hebrew, i. e., with ordinary consonants ַ is the rule, although ִ will be found occasionally, as (the forms marked with † are isolated examples standing for themselves only, while the others represent types) זִכְרִי Ex. 3, 15; דִּבְרֵיכֶם Deut. 5, 25; דִּבְרָתִי Ps. 110, 4 (cf. below, § 59); בִּדְבַר I Ki. 13, 1; מֵינִקְתָּהּ † Gen. 24, 59; מִזְבַּח II Ki. 18, 22; וִירִשְׁתָּהּ † Deut. 17, 14; תִּצְפֹּן Prov. 2, 1; יִדְבַּק Deut. 13, 18; יִגְוַע Job 34, 15; זִכְרוּ Mal. 3, 22; לִמְדוּ Is. 1, 17; מְקַדִּשְׁכֶם † Ex. 31, 13; וְהִתְגַּדִּלְתִּי וְהִתְקַדִּשְׁתִּי † Ezek.

28, 23; וְהִתְקַדִּשְׁתֶּם† Lev. 11, 44; but מְלַמֶּדְךָ Is. 48, 17; יֶדְכֶם Gen. 9, 2; שְׁכֶנְתָּהּ Ex. 3, 22; יְסֹבְבֶנְהוּ Deut. 32, 10; וַתֵּלֶד Gen. 4, 1; יְהַלֶּל־פִּי Ps. 63, 6; נֶגְדִּי Ps. 38, 11; נֶכְדִּי Gen. 21, 23; לֶכְתִּי I Kings 2, 8. Before and after א, ה, ח, ע, ֶ is more common, although there are examples with ִ, which in certain types is the rule: בֶּאֱרוֹת* inferred from בֶּאֱרוֹת Gen. 14, 10; אֶצְלוֹ I Sam. 17, 30; אֶזְרָח Lev. 19, 34; אֶשְׁפֹּט Ps. 75, 3; אֶשְׁקוֹטָה Is. 18, 4; אֶשְׂבַּע Prov. 30, 9; אֶשְׁתֶּה Ps. 50, 13; אֶתְחַבֵּר† II Chron. 20, 35; but אִמְרוֹ† Job 20, 29; אִמְרוּ Is. 3, 10;—יֶהְדֹּף Prov. 10, 3; תֶּהְדַּר Ex. 23, 3; בְּהֶמְתְּךָ Lev. 19, 19; but יִהְיֶה and יִחְיֶה and their like; הֶרְגוּ Num. 25, 5; so always in the prefix הִת־;—יִתְפַּצּוּ Ps. 68, 31; נֶחְשַׁב Num. 18, 27; הֶחְסִיר Ex. 16, 18; חֶלְקוֹ Hab. 1, 16; but חִנָּם Prov. 1, 11; הִנֵּה Gen. 24, 13; חִדְלוּ Is. 2, 22;—נֶעְבַּד Ecc. 5, 8; הֶעְדִּיף Ex. 16, 18; עֶזְרִי Ex. 18, 4; but עִבְדוּ Ex. 5, 18; עִמִּי Gen. 31, 31. Note הֶרְאֲךָ Deut. 4, 36, but הִרְאַנִי Amos 7, 1. In Syriac nothing but ܶ is found.

Sometimes in BA an original ִ may become ֶ, e. g., גֶּשְׁמֵיהוֹן 3, 28 (Syr. ܓܘܫܡܐ, Nöldeke, § 103); the Arabic جِسْمٌ, however, proves that the modification of the vowel occurred outside of Hebrew and is, therefore, not due in Aramaic to Hebrew influence. A similar example in Hebrew is אַתֶּם (BA אַנְתּוּן).

[7] *a* improper, i. e., the *a* which takes the place of a Semitic *i*, is the rule in BA before laryngeals and ר, e. g., פְּלַח 6, 17; הִשְׁתְּכַח 2, 35; מִתְנַצַּח 6, 4; הוֹדַע 2, 15; הַדַּרְתְּ 5, 23; יְמַגַּר 6, 12; it then remains also in an open accented syllable, e. g., שַׁבַּחוּ 5, 4; הַשְׁכַּחוּ 6, 12; אַתַּרוּ 4, 11. Before other consonants there are no examples of *a* improper; the participles מִתְנַדַּב Ez. 7, 13; מִתְעָרַב 2, 43; מִשְׂתַּכַּל 7, 8 seem to be due to the influence of the imperfect (contrast Arabic يَتَقَتَّلُ but مُتَقَتِّلٌ). In Hebrew *a* improper is very frequent, both when the neighbor of a laryngeal and in the environment of other consonants, e. g., גֹּאַלְךָ Is. 48, 17; מִזְבַּחֲךָ I Ki. 8, 31 (for מִזְבֵּחֲךָ); שָׁמַע Gen. 16, 11 (Arabic سَمِعَ); יִשָּׁמַע Ex. 23, 13; תְּשַׁלַּח Ps. 104, 30; הֲנֹטַע אֹזֶן Ps. 94, 9; רֹגַע הַיָּם Is. 51, 15; גָּבַר Ps. 103, 11; גִּדַּל Jos. 4, 14, etc. *a* improper in Hebrew is never found in an open syllable and very rarely in a closed accented syllable in pause (the absolute state of nouns being regarded as a semi-pausal form).

[8] E. g., נְגַד 7, 10; קַבֵּל 6, 1; מְהַלֵּךְ 4, 26; הַנְפֵּק 5, 2; הַשְׁלֵם Ez. 7, 19; יִתְיְהֵב 4, 13, etc.; עִלָּא 6, 3; יְכֵלְתְּ 2, 47. In Hebrew ֵ is the rule in pausal verbal forms and in the absolute state of nouns in

the singular. ֶ in the place of ֵ is found occasionally both in BA and Hebrew, especially before ל, e. g., פַּרְזֶל 2, 33, Heb. בַּרְזֶל Deut. 33, 25. ִ is retained in BA in the accented closed syllable in forms like יְכִל 6, 21; מַלִּל 6, 22; יְמַלִּל 7, 25, etc. No example is available in Hebrew. According to Nöldeke (§ 47) a short *e* may have been lengthened by the tone in Syriac in final syllables, so perhaps in ܢܶܦܶܫ, ܩܶܛܠܶܬ, in which words the Eastern Syrians represent the second vowel by ֵ. The lengthening is nevertheless uncertain, nor do we know whether it was general. Cf. also Wright, *Comp. Gr.*, 84; Zimmern, § 21.

[9] E. g., קַבֵּל 6, 1; עַמָּא Ez. 7, 13, etc. Cf. Hebrew עַמִּי Micah 6, 5, etc. ܥܰܡܳܐ (Nöldeke, § 102), etc.

[10] E. g., אַתְרֵהּ Ez. 5, 15, etc. Cf. Hebrew עַבְדֶּךָ I Ki. 2, 38., etc. Cf. Syriac ܢܥܡܳܐ (Nöldeke, § 94).

[11] Here BA and Hebrew separate. In BA ַ remains (ָ occurs occasionally in pause, as קָדָמָֽי Ez. 4, 18; חָֽיִל Ez. 4, 23; שָׁמְרָֽיִן Ez. 4, 17), e. g., נְפַל 4, 28; אֲזַל, 2, 17, etc., while in Hebrew ָ is the rule in pausal forms and in the absolute singular of nouns, e. g., פָּתָח Ps. 78, 23; בָּשָׂר Gen. 6, 12, etc.

[12] The column "near" exists really only for the Hebrew, since it is a peculiarity of Aramaic that it treats "near" syllables as "distant," so much so that similar treatment in Hebrew is spoken of as an Aramaism (cf. below, § 60). Nevertheless, there are certain types of forms in BA which retain the vowel in an open unaccented syllable immediately before the accent, e. g., فَعَلَة forms, which Barth (§ 92) regards as developed from the فَعِيل infinitive in accordance with his law of compensation, as עֵטָא 2, 14. The ֵ becomes then stationary even in "distant" syllables; hence גְּזֵרַת 4, 14; יְקֵדַת 7, 11; לְחֵנָתָךְ 5, 23; לְחֵנָתֵהּ 5, 2; (שְׁאֵֽלְתָא 4, 14; שְׁלֵֽוְתָךְ 4, 24 in an unaccented closed syllable with metheg). In Hebrew these forms often retain the ֵ, though the accent be shifted, as אֲבֵדַת Deut. 22, 3; בְּרֵכַת II Sam. 2, 13; נְבֵלָתִי Is. 26, 19. No examples are available in Syriac. Other cases are also to be accounted for; firstly, מָזוֹן 4, 9 (cf. Heb. מָזוֹן; cf. above, § 45). Similar forms are found in O. T. Hebrew mostly from verbs ע״ע, e. g., מָגִנִּים I Ki. 10, 17 (from מָגֵן); cstr. st. מָסַךְ Is. 22, 8 (from מָסָךְ); מָעֻזִּים Dan. 11, 38 (from מָעוֹז; while מָעוֹז, cf. Arabic مَعَاذ Sūra 12, 33, really comes from עוז, the Masora seems to derive it from עזז. See GK., § 85). In Syriac we have

ܡܰܥܡܽܘܪܳܐ (cf. Heb. מָקוֹר); ܡܚܘܙܐ regarded by Nöldeke (§ 126 G) as borrowed from the Assyrian (*maḫāzu*, e. g., *ma-ḫa-ze rabūti*, Shalm. Obel. 81); Hebrew מָחוֹז Ps. 107, 30 is likewise a loan-word, and the Syriac word is probably borrowed from the Hebrew and only indirectly from the Assyrian). ܡܳܡܽܘܢܳܐ, although not in O. T. Hebrew, is found in Sirach 31, 8. Nöldeke, *ZAW.*, XXII (1902), 84, doubts the genuineness of the word; LXX has *χρυσίου*; it is very frequent in Mishnaic Hebrew, e. g., Sanhedrin 1, 1). The word occurs also in the N. T. (Mt. 6, 24; 16, 9. 11. 13); while the uncial MSS. all have *μαμμων*, the other spelling (with one *μ*) is attested by versions and patristic citations. מָמוֹן would be parallel to מָכוֹן, just as Syr. ܡܰܓܶܢ (part. of Aph'el) is parallel to Hebrew מָגֵן (see Nestle, *EB.*, col. 2914, § 3; cf. also Lagarde, *Übersicht*, 185). Nöldeke (*Mand.* 130, n. 4) is inclined to regard *mā-* as a very ancient form of the prefix; but his grounds are insufficient. מָזוֹן and its like are rather Hebrew loan-words in Aramaic, and the Hebrew ָ is retained as stationary (cf., on the other hand, מְדֹרָךְ 4, 22). The other cases are the Haph'el forms יְהָקִים 5, 21; 6, 16 (contrast יְקִים 2, 44); מְהָקֵים 2, 21; מָרִים 5, 9; and תְּסֻף 2, 44. Baer (Dan., p. xxxvi) derives תְּסֻף from the root אסף; Kautzsch, though deriving it correctly from סוף, is doubtful as to the certainty of the derivation. It may be questioned, however, whether these are examples of the so-called "lengthening" of a vowel before the tone as in Hebrew, or whether the "lengthening" is not an attempt to increase the volume of the biconsonantal (so-called ע"ו) stem, just as doubling increases the volume of the biconsonantal (so-called ע"ע) stem in תַּדִּק and מְהַדִּק. These forms would then be parallel, as יְתִב and יֵשֵׁב are parallel. In the treatment of verbs ע"ו the Syriac is not always uniform; in some verbs the first radical is doubled after the preformative, e. g., ܐܰܦܶܩ, ܐܰܥܶܠ, etc., while in others the syllable remains open, e. g., ܐܰܩܶܡ, ܐܰܪܶܡ, etc. The general principle in Syriac is that short vowels in open syllables are reduced, but before a consonant originally doubled the short vowel remains even when the doubling is lost and the syllable becomes opened. Occasionally the lost doubling is compensated for in pronunciation by lengthening the vowel. The Eastern Syrians also lengthen short vowels when they remain by way of exception in open syllables, e. g., ܐܘܟܡܬܗ for ܐܘܟܡܬܗ (see Nöldeke, §§ 117 D, and 42).

[13] E. g., הֲקִימַת 7, 4 (cf. Arab. أُقِيمَتْ); אֱלָהּ 2, 18 (cf. Arab. إِلَاهٌ); הֲקִימֵהּ 5, 11 (cf. Hebrew הֱקִיצֹתִי Jer. 31, 26 (25); עֲרָדַיָּא 5, 1 cf. Heb. עָרוֹד Job 39, 5). In Hebrew: חֳדָשָׁיו Job 14, 5; אֱלֹהִים

Gen. 1, 1; עֲבָדַיִךְ I Ki. 5, 4 (sing. עֲבַר); הֲרָרֶיהָ Deut. 8, 9. In Syriac we meet with ܐܶܡܰܪ, ܐܶܡܰܪ, ܐܶܟܰܠ, ܐܶܬܦܬܚ (Nöldeke, § 34); the vowels very probably correspond to the חֲטֵפִין in BA and Hebrew.

[14] E. g., כְּתָב Ez. 7, 22 (Arabic كِتَابٌ); שְׁלָם Ez. 4, 17 (Arabic سَلَامٌ). In Hebrew: שָׁלוֹם Gen. 37, 14, etc. Syriac: ܫܠܳܡܳܐ, etc.

[15] E. g., חֵלֶם 4, 2; מֶלֶךְ 2, 10; אֲכַלִי 7, 5; סִלְקוּ 2, 29; כְּתַבוּ Ez. 4, 8; הַעֵל 5, 13; מִחַן 4, 24; תַּחַת Ez. 6, 5; אֱחָיךְ Ez. 7, 18; בָּרֵךְ 2, 19. In Hebrew: קֹדֶשׁ Jer. 2, 3; רָחָץ Prov. 30, 12; חֵלֶק Gen. 31, 14; נִחַל Ezek. 25, 3; מָוֶת Ex. 10, 17; בַּיִת Deut. 8, 12; אֶבֶן Gen. 29, 2; אֲחַל Ezek. 39, 7. In Syriac ܡܲܠܟܵܐ, ܢܲܦܫܵܐ, ܡܲܠܟܵܐ, etc., prove earlier ܡܲܠܟܵܐ, ܢܲܦܫܵܐ, ܡܲܠܟܵܐ, etc.

47. In BA, as in Hebrew, the consonant of the prefix of the imperf. 3d pers. is י, whereas in Syriac it is ܢ. The BA י, however, is not due to Hebrew influence, as it appears also in the inscriptions.[a] Of course, it is not confined to Hebrew and Aramaic, but is common Semitic, the Syriac standing alone with its ܢ.[b]

[a] Cf. Lidzbarski, 400 ff. It is worthy of note that in the Zenjirli-Hadad inscription three forms occur with ל, viz., למנע line 24, לכתשה and לכתשנה line 31, with which compare BA לֶהֱוֵא 2, 20, etc., לֶהֱוֹן 2, 43, etc., לֶהֶוְיָן 5, 17. On the origin of the ל-prefix and its relation to Arabic لِ expressing purpose, as well as to Syriac ܢ, see König, "Das ל Jaqtul in Semitischen," *ZDMG.*, LI (1897), 330 ff., where he reviews the question with due attention to the opinion of his predecessors.

[b] See Driver, *Tenses*, 7 ff.

48. Since the Syriac does not show the development of internal passives, at least not to the same extent as Hebrew, but uses regularly instead the reflexives with the prefixed ܐܬ, it has been claimed that the Hoph'al forms occurring in BA are due to Hebrew influence (Luzzatto, § 43; Kautzsch, § 34, and contrast § 45, 1, *e;* Blake, *JAOS.*, XXII [1901], 46; Duval, *REJ.*, VIII [1884], 58; on the other side are found Nöldeke, *GGA*, 1867, No. 45, p. 1784; 1884, No. 26, p. 1015; Bevan, 37, note; Behrmann, p. vii).

By the term Hoph'al we mean the internal passive of the Haph'el, corresponding to the Arabic IV. and to the Hebrew Hiph'il. The forms found in BA are as follows: הָנְחַת 5, 20; הָתְקְנַת 4, 33; הוּבַד 7, 11; הוּסְפַת 4, 33; הֳקִימַת 7, 4; הֻעַל 5, 13; הֻעַלוּ 5, 15; הֻסַּק 6, 24; הָחָרְבַת Ez. 4, 15; to which must be added הֵיתָיִת 6, 18 and הֵיתָיוּ 3, 13, and the participle מְהֵימַן 2 A, 45; 6, 5.

There is nothing inherently impossible in the development of an internal passive in BA; and although it has disappeared from the later Aramaic dialects (except perhaps in Palmyrene, cf. Sachau, *ZDMG.*, XXXVII [1883]; 563 f., his vocalization, however, is wrong in the imperf. and participial forms; see below, § 49, n. 2; the readings proposed by Duval, *loc. cit.*, 60 ff., are not convincing; with Sachau agrees D. H. Müller, quoted by Duval in the article referred to, p. 63), traces of it still remain in the so-called passive participles in all Aramaic dialects (including Syriac). The first vowel in the forms quoted above ought certainly to present no difficulties, as it is in agreement with Arabic.

49. The difficulty in these forms seems to be in the ַ as the stem-vowel of the perfect, e. g., הוּבַד. Contrast the Arabic أُقْتِلَ, and on the other hand cf. Hebrew הָקְטַל. Hence, where this agreement with Hebrew is wanting, as in the form הֳקִימַת Arab. أُقِيمَتْ against Hebrew הוּקַם, Jer. 35, 14, even those scholars who, like Kautzsch, look upon the other Hoph'al forms in BA as Hebraisms, admit that we have genuine Aramaic forms ("eine sicher altaramäische Bildung," *GBA.*, § 45, 1, *e;* cf. Bevan, 121). The discrepancy between Arabic, on the one hand, and Hebrew and Aramaic, on the other, with reference to the stem-vowel of the perfect is found, however, also in the active of the Haph'el and Pa'el. The vowel ē in these forms is certainly not due to Hebrew influence, as the same vowel is used in the Syriac. It seems therefore that in Aramaic, independently of Hebrew, during a later period of its history the stem-vowels of the perfect were made to conform to those of the imperfect. The same analogical force was operative in the passive of the causative, i. e., the ַ in הוּבַד was introduced from the imperfect יְהוּבַד*. The following table may serve to illustrate the development:

	Arabic	*Early Aramaic	BA	Syriac	Hebrew
			II or Pa'el Stem		
Perf.....	قَتَّلَ	קַטֵּל	קַטֵּל	ܩܰܛܶܠ	קִטֵּל
Impf. ...	يُقَتِّلُ	יְקַטֵּל	יְקַטֵּל	ܢܩܰܛܶܠ	יְקַטֵּל
			IV or Haph'el Stem		
Perf.....	أَقْتَلَ	הַקְטֵל	הַקְטֵל	ܐܰܩܛܶܠ	הִקְטִיל
Impf. ...	يُقْتِلُ	יְהַקְטֵל	יְהַקְטֵל	ܢܰܩܛܶܠ	יַקְטִיל
	for يُؤَقْتِلُ				
			IV Passive or Hoph'al		
Perf.....	أُقْتِلَ	הָקְטַל	הָקְטַל		הָקְטַל
Impf. ...	يُقْتَلُ	יְהַקְטַל	יְהָקְטַל		יָקְטַל
Part.....	مُقْتَلٌ	מְהַקְטַל	מְהָקְטַל	ܡܩܰܛܰܠ	מָקְטָל
			מְהֵימַן		

(1) In the case of הֵיתָיִת and הֵיתָיִו the influence of the imperfect upon the perfect may have gone a step farther and changed the first vowel as well as the second. Or else הֵיתִי was regarded by the language as a فَيْعَلَ; cf. the passive of فَوْعَلَ forms in Hebrew כּוֹנְנוּ Ps. 67, 23, with the active כּוֹנֵן Ps. 9, 8. The vocalization הֵיתָיו (for הֵיתוֹ) goes with that of Hebrew forms like חָסָיוּ Deut. 32, 37 (for חָסוּ Ps. 37, 40).

(2) Sachau, *loc. cit.*, although probably right in considering the Palmyrene forms adduced there as passives, errs in their vocalization. He is misled by Arabic يُقْتَلُ, مُقْتَلٌ and Hebrew יָקְטַל, מָקְטָל. In these forms, however, the ָ represent the vowel of the prefix which remained, while the vowel following the syncopated ا (ה; cf. above, § 28) was dropped. That vowel was ַ, as may be proved from the analogy of the passive of the II (Aram. Pa'el). Thus we have يُقَتَّلُ, مُقَتَّلٌ, cf. Syr. ܡܩܰܛܰܠ (Nöldeke, § 165). Hence, the impf. passive of the Pa'el had the form יְקַטַּל (active יְקַטֵּל). Its perf. was originally קֻטַּל and later (through the influence of the impf.) it became קֻטֵּל.

In the same manner, from the part. caus. pass. we are able to reconstruct the imperf., from מְקַטַּל (ܡܩܛܠ Nöld., *loc. cit.*)—יְהַקְטַל, יְקַטַל. On the subject of internal passives in the Semitic languages and their gradual disappearance, cf. Nöldeke, *Mand.*, § 162; Wright, *Comp. Gr.*, 226, 253; König, *Lehrgeb.*, II, 384 f.; Vollers-Burkitt, § 42.

50. The forms אֶשְׁתּוֹמַם Dan. 4, 16 and מְסוֹבְלִין Ez. 6, 3 are also in apparent agreement with the Hebrew. On אשתומם Bevan (p. 93) says it "is a hybrid form based on the Hebrew הִשְׁתּוֹמֵם (cf. וָאֶשְׁתּוֹמֵם Dan. 8, 27), with change of the ה to א after the analogy of the later Jewish Aramaic." With respect to מְסוֹבְלִין Driver and Cheyne (Variorum Bible) regard the text as doubtful. Kautzsch (§ 36) says that both forms are probably Hebraisms.

Wright explains מְסוֹבְלִין on the analogy of the Arabic III. فَاعَلَ, *ā* becoming *ō*. This form "is in general use in Arabic only, but examples occur in Ethiopic, too . . . . The inflexion runs entirely parallel to that of the intensive form . . . ." (*Comp. Gr.*, pp. 202 f.).

We cannot, however, regard these forms as clear examples of the Arabic III فَاعَلَ, for that stem always carries with it the reciprocal idea. As Wright declares, it "expresses an effort, with the implied idea of a counter-effort" (*Comp. Gr.*, p. 202), and "the ideas of effort and reciprocity are always more or less clearly implied" (*Arab. Gr.*, I, 33 D). Since the meaning peculiar to the Arabic III is absent from these words, we must regard them as examples of the فَوْعَلَ form, which appears in Ethiopic and Syriac, although it is rare in Arabic. Thus Duval (*Syr. Gram.*, § 197) cites several examples in Syriac, as: ܫܘܫܪ more frequently ܫܡܫܪ, ܗܘܓܠ, ܫܘܠܦ, ܟܘܬܪ, and ܐܙܕܘܓܠ. These verbs are also used in the passives. Cf. Payne Smith, who regards ܫܘܓܪ mentioned by Duval as a Shaph'el form of ܓܪ, together with its passive as an Eshtaph'al. Cf. also Praetorius, *Aeth. Gram.*, 37, where he adds examples in Arabic, as ضَيْغَمٌ and فَيْصَلٌ.

In these forms, as in רוֹמַם, the *ō* represents an original *au*, and not *ā*, as Wright has it. The true character of the forms was recognized, as far back as 1876, by Nöldeke who says (*ZDMG.*, XXIX

[1876], 326): "Bildungen wie הִתְגּוֹלֵל sind auch aramäisch, vergl. ܐܶܬܬܰܘܗܰܪ Athan. 29, 3; Efr. 1, 439 D, u. s. w., ܐܶܬܓܰܘܪܰܪ, ܐܶܬܦܰܘܪܰܪ BA 7323. Demnach brauchen wir אשתומם in Daniel ebensowenig als Hebraismus anzusehen wie so manche andere Bildung im Biblisch.-Aram., bei der eine solche Annahme nahe zu liegen scheint." Haupt, in *SBOT.*, Ezra, pp. 36 f., derives מְסוֹבְלִין from סבל ("*to carry*") a synonym of הוּבַל.

51. Verbal forms in BA which agree with Hebrew are מְרוֹמֵם 4, 34, and הִתְרוֹמַמְתָּ 5, 23. Kautzsch (§ 45, 6) regards these as Hebraized forms, and Bevan (p. 97) says that the forms "are, of course, borrowed from the Hebrew; the verb רוֹמֵם '*to exalt*' occurs again in the Targums and in Christian Palestinian, which shows that it had really passed into common use." Kautzsch, however, classifies the forms correctly, calling them "Pa'lel and Hithpa'lel" (Hithpa'lal?) respectively. Stade (*Heb. Gram.*, § 155, *c*) likewise correctly explains such forms in Hebrew by placing קוֹמֵם forms by the side of שַׁאֲנַן and נָאוָה; but he then claims that the *ō* represents *ā* (similarly GK., § 72, 7), thus being guilty of a contradiction, for שַׁאֲנַן, נָאוָה; i. e., שַׁאֲנַן*, נַאֲוָה* are clearly פַּעְלַל forms, while קוֹמֵם *ḳāmim*(*a*), i. e., *kām-am*(*a*) would have to be designated as a فَعَلَّل form—which, of course, is an impossibility. In a footnote, Stade says that the Syriac *au* in these forms is probably a resolution of *ō*. Syriac *au* is rather the original, which in BA and Hebrew in accordance with rule becomes contracted into *ō*.

Similar forms appear in Syriac, as ܐܶܬܓܰܘܪܰܪ "*to chew the cud, to meditate,*" ܐܶܬܬܰܘܗܰܪ "*to be amazed,*" ܦܰܘܪܰܪ "*to break in pieces,*" ܐܶܬܦܰܘܪܰܪ "*to be crumbled in pieces,*" ܦܰܘܪܰܪ, ܐܶܬܦܰܘܪܰܪ with similar meanings, and ܐܶܬܬܰܘܗܰܪ "*to be amazed*" (from ܬܘܗ; Nöldeke, § 180). In Arabic there is a form فَعْلُولَةٌ in verbs middle و and ى in which the second radical always becomes ى. Thus دَيْمُومَةٌ from دوم, كَيْنُونَةٌ from كون. Wright says that "the rare substantive forms سُودَدٌ from ساد '*to be chief or ruler,*' and عَوْطَطٌ from عاط '*to desire the male of a camel;*'" certain cognate forms; "and the analogy of the Aramaic verbal form פַּעְלֵל (as ܦܘܼܪܣ, ܦܘܼܪܙܙ) and the Hebrew פַּעְלֵל (as בּוֹנֵן, קוֹמֵם, etc.) all combine to prove that فَعْلُوَةٌ comes directly from a quadriliteral فَعْلَلَ (*Arab. Gram.*, I, 120 D; *Comp. Gram.*, 203 f.).

These forms are all analogous:

Arabic	Syriac	BA	Hebrew
فَعْلَلَ	ܦܘܼܪܣ	(רַוְמֵם) רוֹמֵם	רוֹמֵם
	ܐܬܦܪܣܘܣ	הִתְרוֹמַמְתָּ	

52. We have in BA forms like אֶבֶן, חֵלֶם, etc., which are found also in Hebrew. In BA they are found by the side of forms which are rare in Hebrew, such as לְחֶם, צְלֵם, etc. It is customary to speak of לְחֶם forms in Hebrew as Aramaisms, and of אֶבֶן forms in BA as Hebraisms. (So, e. g., Kautzsch, *GBA.*, § 54, 1; Merx, *Trans. Orient. Cong. Berlin*, I, p. 159.)

These so-called "segolate" forms found in BA are as follows:

אֶבֶן 2, 34; 6. 18; Ez. 5, 8; 6, 4; אֶלֶּה 7, 10; חֲוֹל 3, 4. 20; חֵלֶם 7, 1; טַעַם Ez. 6, 14; מֶלֶךְ 2, 10. 37; 4, 34; 7, 1; Ez. 5, 11. 12; 6, 12. 14; 7, 11. 12; נֶגֶד 6, 11; צֶלֶם 3, 5. 7. 10. 12. 14. 18; קַיִט 2, 35; קֶרֶן 7. 8. Cf. also the following, אִתְגְּזֶרֶת 2, 45; הִתְגְּזֶרֶת 2, 34; כְּעֶנֶת Ez. 4, 10. 11; 7, 12 parallel to כְּעֶת Ez. 4, 17; פַּרְשֶׁגֶן Ez. 4, 11. 23, 5, 6; 7, 11; הַשְׁכַּחַת 2, 25; הִשְׁתְּכַחַת 5, 27; (cf. also perf. 3 f. s. הִשְׁתְּכַחַת 5, 11. 12. 14; 6, 5. 23).

It is necessary for us to know something of the origin of "segolate" forms in order to decide whether they are common to several of the Semitic languages, and also whether they are to be classified on statistic grounds or on grounds of internal grammatical growth. (The term "segolate" is usually restricted to nouns, but it may be applied likewise to verbal formations.) A "segolate" noun may be defined as a noun with a vowel between the first and second radicals of the basic forms, and none between the second and third; i. e., it is of the form cvcc –. When we speak of "segolates," we refer to Semitic nouns, and not to Hebrew or Aramaic formations, because the absence of a vowel between the second and third radicals in Aramaic is no guarantee of its absence in Semitic times. (Thus צִדְקָה Dan. 4, 24 could not be determined to be a non-"segolate" without the aid of Hebrew צְדָקָה.) Hence, if we had only Aramaic, we should not know in any given case whether we had "segolate" formations or not. We determine Aramaic "segolates," therefore, by the aid of Hebrew or Arabic.

It is to be observed (1) that the various nominal forms in the several Semitic languages do not necessarily correspond; (2) that in Hebrew itself "segolate" and non-"segolate" forms interchange; e. g., כָּתֵף Zech. 7, 11; כֶּתֶף I Ki. 6, 8; יָרֵךְ Jud. 15, 8; יֶרֶךְ Gen. 24, 9; גָּדֵר Num. 22, 24; גֶּדֶר Prov. 24, 31, etc. Lagarde, therefore, seems to be right when he claims that in Hebrew there are proper and improper "segolates." The former come from Semitic times; the latter were developed within Hebrew itself. Therefore with each "segolate" form the question must be asked: Is it a proper or an improper form? Moreover, while it is true that there were proper "segolates" in Semitic times, it is plain that they also go back to fuller dissyllabic forms, the second stem-vowel being lost in accordance with early Semitic accentuation.

So much for the basis in forms like אַבְנִי, מַלְכִּי, etc. But in forms like אַבְנְכוֹן, no matter whether in its origin it be a proper or improper "segolate," the question is whether it is not possible that there was another pronunciation, i. e., אֲבֶנְכוֹן, in which ֶ might have been simply a parasitic vowel. (This depends, however, upon the collocation of consonants. No parasitic vowel would intrude in a form like מַלְכְּכוֹן, because the latter is pronounceable, while in אַבְנְכוֹן the vowel would be necessary.) By dropping the suffix from this form we have the construct state of the noun אֲבַן or אֲבֶן.

The form אֶבֶן in Hebrew is the construct state of "segolates." It presupposes אַבְנְכוֹן, which is not found in Hebrew, but is a legitimate form in Syriac, produced by reading with

ܡܗܝܡܢܐ (on ܡܗܝܡܢܐ see Nöldeke, §§ 17, 34, 52 C; Brockelmann, § 12). Hence for their existence in BA no Hebrew influence whatever need be assumed.

A "segolate" therefore is a form which, in the basic form, has a silent *shewa* under the second radical, if that *shewa* be Semitic. When in the course of inflection that *shewa* is followed by a so-called vocal *shewa*, then it may be pronounced hurriedly (*marheṭānā*) or slowly (*mehaggiānā*), and the latter pronunciation yields a "segolate" formation.

The following table of forms will illustrate the development:

	מַדְנַח	פָּעְלֵי	נַעְרֵי	יַגְלֵי	אַבְנֵי
Marheṭana	מַדְנְחָאֵי	פָּעְלְכֶם	נַעְרְכֶם	יַגְלְכֶם	אַבְנְכֶם
Mehaggiana	מְדִינְחָאֵי[b]	{ פָּעֳלְכֶם פְּעַלְכֶם.	נַעֲרְכֶם[a]	יְגֶלְכֶם	אֱבֶנְכֶם
		פֹּעַל	נַעַר	יֶגֶל	אֶבֶן

[a] So in Jewish Aramaic מַעֲרְבָאֵי.

[b] Jewish Aramaic.

In the light of these forms it is not astonishing to find that so-called "segolate" formations are found in Christian Palestinian; e. g., מילך, מישך (pronounced מֶשֶׁךְ or מֵשֶׁךְ). So also in the Peshiṭta ܐܘܪܚ *'uraḥ* (from primitive *'urḥ*). See Nöldeke, *ZDMG.*, XXII (1868), p. 475. On the ground of these forms Bevan (*Commentary*, p. 71) and Behrmann (*Commentary*, p. viii) consider it doubtful whether אֶבֶן forms in BA are to be regarded as Hebraisms. Behrmann, however, while admitting that the noun forms may be original, regards the "segolate" verb formations as Hebraisms of the Masora. The same pronunciation, however, which produced the segolate noun-formation would also operate in verb-forms; e. g., קְטַלְתּוּן or קְטַלְתּוּן (cf. בְּנֵיתַהּ Dan. 4, 27) קְטַלְתּוּן, קִטְלֶת, similarly אֲמֶרֶת. It need not be supposed that the forms are made anew in each case. When once the type is introduced, other forms are made by analogy. (On the general subject of segolates cf. GK., 84, *a;* König, *Lehrgeb.*, II; Lambert, *RÉJ.*, 1896, pp. 18 ff.; Lagarde, *Übersicht*, pp. 72 f. and 80 f.; *Mittheil.*, I, p. 150; Philippi, *Beiträge z. Assyr.*, II, pp. 359–389; Ungnad, *ZA.*, XVII [1903], pp. 333 f.)

53. In BA the dual appears in certain forms, יְדַיִן (in בִּידַיִן) 2, 34; מָאתַיִן Ez. 6, 17; קַרְנַיִן 7, 7; רַגְלַיִן 7, 4; שִׁנַּיִן 7, 7.

Marti (*GBA.*, p. 73) cites also the following: תְּרֵי, תַּרְתֵּין and עַיְנַיִן 7, 8; עִדָּנִין 7, 25, and פַּרְסִין 5, 25. In the use of the dual, BA represents an older stage of language than does the Syriac. In the latter, while a few traces of the dual still exist (in two or three words, viz.: ܬܪ̈ܝܢ, f. ܬܪ̈ܬܝܢ [cf. BA תַּרְתֵּין above]; ܡܐܬܝܢ [cf. BA מָאתַיִן]; and ܥܣܪ̈ܝܢ), yet it had disappeared as a component part of the language (cf. Nöldeke, § 70, n.). Indeed, the tendency in all the Semitic languages seems to be to discard the dual. Traces of it are found also in Ethiopic and Assyrian; and it survives to a limited extent in Modern Arabic (cf. Vollers and Burkitt, p. 106; Wright, *Comp. Gr.*, 149 f.; Zimmern, 173; König, *Heb. und Sem.*, 49).

In the inscriptions, Lidzbarski (p. 397) is able to identify as duals only the Nabatean forms תריין, תרתין and מאתין, and the Palmyrene תרתן.

B. AGREEMENTS BETWEEN BA AND HEBREW OCCASIONED BY THE FACT OF THEIR RELATIONSHIP WITHIN THE CLASS OF SEMITIC LANGUAGES

54. Most of these agreements have been discussed in connection with the preceding sections. Cf. especially, §§ 8–11, on the origin of ה and א in the ending of feminine nouns and of nouns in the emphatic state, and in the prefix of verbal forms; 16–25, on consonantal doubling and the assimilation of נ; 26–27, on transposition of consonants; 28–31, on syncope of ה; 35, on the peculiarities of the laryngeals; 36–40, on quiescent א; 43, on the treatment of ו and י; 44–46, on the vocalization; 48, on the prefix י in the imperfect; 48–51, on the Hoph'al and other verb forms; 52, on segolates; 53, on the dual.

C. AGREEMENTS BETWEEN BA AND HEBREW DUE TO ARAMAIC INFLUENCE UPON HEBREW

55. The BA doubles the first radical in forms from ע״ע roots after a formative prefix;[a] when there is no prefix, the second radical receives the doubling;[b] occasionally the latter method is also used in the former case. The first method is so peculiarly Aramaic that, wherever it occurs in Hebrew, we speak of it there as an Aramaism (GK., § 67 *g*; Margolis, *AJSL.*, XII [1896], 213). The examples are:

a) Pe'al, imperf. תֵּרֹעַ 2, 40 with rejection of *d. forte* from ר; inf. מִחַן (Syr. ܡܶܚܰܢ) 4, 24; Haph'el, perf. 3 m. s. הַנְעֵל (Syr. ܐܰܥܶܠ) 2, 25; 6, 19, with resolution of doubling by insertion of Nun; 3 f. s. הַדֶּקֶת (Syr. ܐܰܕܶܩܬ) 2, 34. 45; 3 m. pl. הַדִּקוּ (Syr. ܐܰܕܶܩܘ) 6, 25; imperf. 3 f. s. תַּדִּק (Syr. ܬܰܕܶܩ) 2, 40. 44; 2 f. s. with suff. תַּדֻּקִנַּהּ 7, 23; imperative 2. m. s. with suff. הַעֲלְנִי (for an explanation of the form cf. Margolis, *AJSL.*, XIX [1902], 45–48) 2, 24; inf. הַעָלָה 5, 7 and with resolution of doubling by insertion of Nun הַנְעָלָה 4, 3; part. m. מְהַדֵּק (Syr. ܡܰܕܶܩ) 2, 40; f. מַדֱּקָה 7, 7. 19; Hoph'al, הֻעַל 5, 13; הֻעַלּוּ 5, 15 (with virtual doubling of the ע; the *d. forte* in ל is similar to that in חָדֵלּוּ Jud. 5, 7; וְיִחֵלּוּ Job 29, 21, etc. In Hebrew, however, all these examples are in pause; but the regular Aramaic forms in the 3. plural correspond to the pausal forms in Hebrew; cf. GK., § 20, 2, *c.*). Example of a noun: מֶעָלֵי 6, 15. Kautzsch, § 60, 3, *b*, followed by others, fails to understand the form; מֶעָלֵי however, = מַעֲלֵי* = ܡܰܥܠܶܝ; the variant מֶעָלֵי, on the other hand, = Syr. ܡܶܥܠܳܝ (cf. Behrmann *ad locum*).

b) Pe'al perfect, 3 m. s. עַל (Syr. ܥܰܠ) 2, 16. 24; 4, 5; 6, 11; 3 f. s. עַלַּת (Syr. ܥܶܠܠܰܬ) 5, 10 ḳ (עללת k); נַדַּת 6, 19; but contrast 3 m. pl. הַדִּקוּ (Syr. ܕܰܩܘ) 2, 35; probably for הַדִּקוּ after ע״ע analogy; impv. pl. m. גֹּדּוּ 4, 11. 20; part. pl. עללין (k) עָלִּין (k) (Syr. ܥܳܐܠܺܝܢ or ܥܳܠܺܝܢ, see Nöldeke, § 178, B) 4, 4; 5, 8. We miss, however, a metheg: עָלִּין cf. בָּתִּין above, § 25. Example of a noun: מְגִלָּה Ez. 6, 2; cf. Syr. ܡܶܓܰܠܬܳܐ, ܡܶܓܰܠܬܳܐ (Nöldeke, § 126 B).

56. Aphæresis, or loss of an initial consonant, takes place in BA in the case of א in the words חַד 3, 19; חֲדָא Ez. 5, 13. In Hebrew the only regular instance appears to be נַחְנוּ for אֲנַחְנוּ (cf. *ZDMG.*, 1876, 707); חַד, Ezek. 33, 30 (see, however, Cornill, 398), may be regarded as an Aramaism. In Syriac ܐ loses its consonantal value in many words, and although written in the text it has the "linea occultans" and is not pronounced; e. g., ܐ̱ܢ̱ܬ, or ܢܬ. In certain words, however, ܐ is always omitted in writing, e. g., ܡܳܢ, exactly as in BA (Nöldeke, § 32). The examples which Kautzsch cites (§ 11, 3, *a*) of the first radical in the imperative of verbs פ״י, e. g., הַב 5, 17; דַּע 6, 16, and of verbs פ״ן, e. g., שָׂא Ez. 5, 15; פְּקוּ 3, 26 are not really examples of aphæresis, if thereby is meant "a

psycho-physiological process, not merely the absence of a letter in front. The imperative being the prefixless 'apocopatus,' the forms mentioned are direct descendants of יְהַב, יְדַע, יִשָּׂא, יִפַּק" (Margolis, *AJSL.*, XIX [1902], 162). This is true of verbs פ״י in Syriac and in Arabic, and of verbs פ״ן in Syriac, as well as in Hebrew (cf. Wright, I, § 144; Nöldeke, §§ 173, 175; GK., §§ 66 *a*, *c*, 69 *b*, *h*).

57. The regular plural ending of masculine nouns in BA is ־ִין. This is also the regular plural in Syriac (cf. Nöldeke, § 70). The Hebrew form מַלְכִין Prov. 31, 3, etc., is called an Aramaism. It illustrates the care necessary in using the term "Hebraism," "Aramaism," etc., which should indicate a form or word or grammatical peculiarity borrowed from one language by the other, but is usually applied in the grammars to a development and use in a less frequent manner of phenomena that are the rule in related languages. Thus, in this case, Kautzsch believes that the use of the plural ending ־ִין in Hebrew is not to be regarded as a pure Aramaism, but as a late weakening ("Abschwächung") of the original ־ִים, and cites as proof the form חמשן "fifty" in l. 28 of the Mesha inscription.

The two instances of the plural ending in ־ִים viz., אֲנָשִׁים 4, 14 and אלפים 7, 10 (k) (אַלְפִין k) are not Hebraisms of the author, but are probably due to the thoughtlessness of some copyist (so Kautzsch, § 51, 2; Behrmann, 28; Kamphausen, *SBOT.*, Daniel, p. 25). So also is the form מַלְכִים, for מַלְכִין Ez. 4, 13, probably a scribal error. It is possible, however, that ם here represents a dialectal variant in Aramaic. It would then be analogous to the use of לְהֹם and לְכֹם Ez. 5, 3 for לְהוֹן 2, 35, and לְכוֹן 3, 4 (cf. also לְהוֹם Jer. 10, 11). The suffix הם occurs frequently in the inscriptions, e. g., להם Zenjirli, Bauin., 18; בטנהם *CIS.*, II, 145, 1; אלהיהם *ibid.*, 2; קימיהם *ibid.*, 3; Nabatean, נפשהם ואחרהם *CIS.*, II, 198, 2; להם *CIS.*, II, 205, 2; בניהם אחרהם *CIS.*, II, 209, ll. 2 and 5, מנהם l. 6; בניהם *CIS.*, II, 158, 4 (see Haupt, *SBOT.*, Ezra 4, 13, where he refers to *Johns Hopkins Univ. Circ.* No. 114, July, 1894, p. 118, *b*).

58. BA בַּאדַיִן 2, 14; רֵאשׁ 2, 38, etc. (cf. Syriac ܪܫܐ) have their parallels in Hebrew רֵאשׁ inferred from רֵאשִׁית Gen. 1, 1, which one is tempted to regard as an Aramaism by the side

of the genuine Hebrew רֵאשׁ (cf. Arabic رَأْسٌ), יֵאמַר Gen. 31, 8, etc., provided the ֵ is explained with Haupt, "The Assyrian E-Vowel," *American Journal of Philology*, October, 1887, pp. 265–291, as *imālah*. Ethiopic *re'(e)s* (*ra's* would have yielded *rō's*; Praetorius, *Äthiop. Gram.*, § 16, 1), as well as Arabic بِئْرٌ and the like, corresponding to Hebrew בְּאֵר Gen. 21, 30; זְאֵב Gen. 49, 27; רְאֵם Num. 23, 22, etc., which Haupt regards as resolutions from בֵּאר, etc., seem to indicate that *ra'š* and *ri'š*, etc., represent from the beginning parallel Semitic forms (cf. also Nöldeke, *Mand.*, 16; Margolis, *AJSL.*, XII [1896], 225; XIV [1903], 162 f.; Sievers, I, 280, n. 2; Haupt, *SBOT.*, Proverbs, p. 34; *ibid.*, Isaiah, p. 88; Jäger, *BSS.*, I, 472).

59. The modification in Hebrew of Semitic *a* to *i*(*e*) in closed (unaccented) syllables, which is common to all Aramaic dialects (cf. above, § 46, n. 6, for BA and Syriac), is considered by Nöldeke (*Mand.*, § 16; cf. *ZDMG.*, XXII [1868], 454) as due to Aramaic influence.

This modification of *a* to *i* and *e* is, however, common to all Semitic languages, although it is most apparent in Hebrew (and therefore in the BA) because of the more exact system of vowel symbols developed by the Masoretes. It is probable that each of the three short vowels varied considerably in pronunciation, from the scarcely audible *shewa* to the so-called tone-long vowels, and that only the paucity of vowel symbols prevented these variations from being represented in writing other Semitic languages. That it is not solely Aramaic or Hebrew is proved by similar variations which occur in the spoken dialects of Modern Arabic (cf. Vollers and Burkitt, 18 ff.; and Zimmern, 39).

60. On what Margolis terms the Aramaic method in Hebrew nominal inflection, cf. *AJSL.*, XII (1896), 213 ff., where the implication is, not that this method was applied to the Hebrew of the Old Testament by the Masoretes who spoke as their vernacular an Aramaic dialect, and were therefore more or less influenced by it in their reading of the Hebrew, but that the Aramaic method is merely the one which is uniformly used in Aramaic, being ultimately based, however, on a phonetic development which had its beginning in Semitic times and

entered Hebrew at a late period, when it crossed with another phonetic development likewise originating in Semitic times (cf. above, § 57).

61. There remain a few cases of agreement between BA and Hebrew which cannot be eliminated by the process employed in our investigation. Most of these, however, are due to mechanical features of the Masora, while some are simply errors.

The BA agrees with Hebrew in the form of the demonstrative pronoun אֵלֶּה, Jer. 10, 11, and אלה (k) אֵל (k) Ez. 5, 15. Both of these may be errors by the copyists, though not necessarily so, for the demonstrative appears in this form in some of the inscriptions; e. g., אל Hadad I, 29; אלה Na., 207, 3 (cf. Lidzbarski, 264).

62. In Hebrew there is no distinction in form between the masc. and fem. of the perf. 3d pl. Similarly, in BA the *kethibh* makes no distinction, but the *kere* everywhere requires קְטַלָה for קטלו; e. g., נפקו, נְפַקָה 5, 5; אתעקרו, אֶתְעֲקַרָה 7, 8; and נפלו, נְפַלָה 7, 20.

The question here is as to which represents the original. Kautzsch (p. 46) suggests that the original did actually distinguish between the genders in the perf. 3d pl., but that this distinction was lost through an Hebraizing textual revision, in which case the *kere* is a restitution of the original. He inclines to the supposition that the non-distinction of gender (due to Hebrew influence) is the original, and that the Masora was the first to introduce the distinction into its system of vocalization, as that distinction was familiar to it from the Targums. Bevan (p. 99 f.) also regards the *kethibh* as the original, but, unlike Kautzsch, he holds that the use of the same form for both genders is not necessarily a Hebraism, but may be due to grammatical laxity, for the same phenomenon appears in Nabatean and Modern Arabic. (Cf. Vollers and Burkitt, 36; *CIS.*, II, 205, 1; Cooke, 221; Wright, *Comp. Gram.*, 169.)

In Ruth 1, 13 הֲלָהֵן may stand for הלהם and is an instance of the same textual laxity, although most commentators take לָהֵן here to mean "therefore" as in BA.

63. In the use of *d. lene* the Masoretes treated BA precisely like Hebrew. The spirants take *d. lene* at the beginning of a syllable unless preceded by a vowel; e. g., חַכִּימֵי בָבֶל 2, 18. Even this, however, may not be due to Hebrew influence, for Syriac has similar phenomena (cf. Nöldeke, *Syr. Gram.*, § 24). The so-called *daghesh lene orthophonicum* is another instance which is simply a mechanical device to secure orthoepy. It was used no doubt to indicate the accurate pronunciation of a word, but was no part of the spoken language. It occurs in קֳדָם־מַלְכָּא 2, 10, and טַעְמָּא 6, 3 (cf. Kautzsch, § 9, Rem. 3; GK., § 13, 2 n.).

64. The use of the so-called *pathaḥ-furtive* is a further instance. It is found in BA in תְּרֵעַ 2, 40; רֵיחַ 3, 27; רוּחַ 4, 5. 6. 15; 5, 11. 12. 14; שְׁלִיחַ 5, 24; Ez. 7, 14; יְדִיעַ 3, 18; Ez. 4, 12. 13; 5. 8. This phonetic phenomenon most probably existed in Syriac and the other Aramaic dialects, but cannot now be discerned because of their less exact system of vowel representation.

65. The forms יוכל 2, 10 and תוכל (k) 5, 16, which are regarded by Kautzsch (§ 43, *b*) and Bevan (p. 39) as Hebraisms, are perhaps scribal errors for יִכֻּל (as in 3, 29), תִּכֻּל (so Behrmann). Cf. the Targumic יְכוֹל; also the Christian Palestinian dialect, in which verbs פ״י often take *ō* in the second syllable of the imperfect (cf. Nöldeke, *ZDMG.*, XXII [1868], 500). Cf. also above, § 41, for יוכל as a possible Aramaic form.

66. The use of ◌ֶ for ◌ֵ in pausal imperfect forms of verbs ל״ה may be a Hebraism; e. g., אֶחַוֶּה 2, 24; נְחַוֶּה 2, 4; נְהַחֲוֶה 2, 7; יְהַחֲוֶה 5, 12. Kautzsch (§ 47, *f*) thinks that it rests upon a theory of the Masora which is just as questionable in Hebrew; cf. וֶחְיֵה Prov. 7, 2 (cf. above, § 6 *e*).

The few instances of ◌ָ for ◌ַ in pause may be part of the Hebraization of the text which we must assume began in late Masoretic times and has crept into certain MSS. and the ordinary editions of our OT. text. Most of these late corruptions have been removed through the efforts of Baer, Ginsburg, and Strack. A few, however, have undoubtedly remained, and are not to be placed to the credit of the early Masora, much less to the living speech in Palestine.

Thus, the supposed Hebraisms in the grammar of the BA are reduced to a minimum which, at best, originates in a certain dialectal variety of Aramaic.

www.ingramcontent.com/pod-product-compliance
Lightning Source LLC
Chambersburg PA
CBHW060430050426
42449CB00009B/2221

* 9 7 8 1 5 5 6 3 5 7 9 8 5 *